The Bouncer™

Sion, a man haunted by a tragic past
Within him lies strength and kindness, but also great sorrow
All this will change when he meets a girl named Dominique
These are the residents of DOG STREET

OFFICIAL STRATEGY GUIDE

BY DAN BIRLEW

THE BOUNCER OFFICIAL STRATEGY GUIDE

LEGAL STUFF

Brady Publishing
An Imprint of
Pearson Education
201 W. 103rd St.
Indianapolis, IN 46290

ISBN: 0-7440-0058-0
Library of Congress No.: 00-136740

Printing Code: The rightmost double-digit number is the year of the book's printing; the rightmost single-digit number is the number of the boo
printing. For example, 01-1 shows that the first printing of the book occurred in 2001.

04 03 02 01   4 3 2 1

AUTHOR ACKNOWLEDGEMENTS

The author wishes to acknowledge the contributions of the folks at
DreamFactory and Squaresoft for their help on this guide. Also, many thanks
and appreciation to Leigh Davis, David Waybright and Tim Cox for their great
suggestions and contributions to the book. Many thunderous handclaps for
the BradyGAMES design and layout crew, who work incredibly hard to make all
the books I write look fantastic. Ken, Ann-Marie, Carol, Bob, Jane, Lisa,
Tracy, Kurt, Dan and Robin, plus anyone else who has contributed to one of
these Squaresoft projects I've worked on. I'd like to extend a special thanks to
my wife Laura, for snapping all of the screenshots contained in this book.

ABOUT THE AUTHOR

Dan Birlew is the author of several BradyGAMES strategy
guides, including such titles as Chrono Cross, Parasite Eve 2
and Final Fantasy IX. He lives in Southern California with his
wife Laura, and has created and maintains Internet websites
dedicated to specific video games.

BRADYGAMES STAFF

Director of Publishing
David Waybright

Editor-In-Chief
H. Leigh Davis

Creative Director
Robin Lasek

Marketing Manager
Janet Eshenour

Licensing Assistant
Mike Degler

CREDITS

Title Manager
Tim Cox

Screen Shot Editor
Michael Owen

Book Designer
Ann-Marie Deets

Production Designers
Bob Klunder
Jane Washburne
Tracy Wehmeyer

Map Design
Mike Heisler for
Idea + Design Works, LLC
www.ideaanddesignworks.com

BradyGAMES would like to thank the talented folks at
Squaresoft for all their support on this book. In particular,
we need to thank Jonathan Williams, Yutaka Sano,
Ryo Taketomi, David Carrillo, Mohammed A. C. Wright,
Fernando Bustamante, Rika Maruya, Jennifer Mukai,
Bryan Chen, Michael Erickson, Richard Honeywood,
and Keiko Kato. We couldn't have done it without you!

We would also like to extend an extra special thanks to
the IGNPS2 staff for their contributions to this book. In
particular, we would like to acknowledge Douglass C. Perry,
David Zdyrko, and David Smith. Thanks for all the help!

Also, we need to thank Ansel Wilson for his superior
translation skills!

ABLE OF CONTENTS

INTRODUCTION

The Bouncer™ is Squaresoft's first bilingual, DVD title to appear on the new PlayStation 2 game console. The game is quite unlike anything that has been done before, and for that reason we have developed a whole new format just for this guide. This section of the book explains how The Bouncer is a completely unique, interactive experience, and how to effectively use this guide to conquer the game like a real pro.

ABOUT THE BOUNCER

The Bouncer is a "3D Action" game, which gives you the sensation of playing a part in an action movie. During the demo movie, press the START button to skip to the Title screen. You can choose from the following three modes of play:

◎ **Story Mode** (1 player) ◎ **Versus Mode** (1-4 players) ◎ **Survival Mode** (1 player)

Story Mode is explored in further detail later in this section. For more information on the other modes, refer to their specific chapters in the b[...]

STORY MODE OVERVIEW

The main mode of the game is the one-player Story Mode. Only by completing Story Mode can the player unlock hidden characters for us[...] Versus and Survival Modes, and strengthen characters while improving and expanding their fighting abilities. The game is played with a t[...] of trained bouncers: Sion Barzahd, Volt Krueger, and Kou Leifoh. The story progresses in a series of **Events** and **Battles**.

EVENTS

Events are cut-scenes and CG animations in which the plot of the game is revealed. Situations will aris[...] and tensions will mount. After the scene ends, the battle ensues.

ACTIVE CHARACTER SELECT

After an Event, you must choose a character to fight as from a selection panel. The bouncer you choose serves as the "leader" in the upcoming fight. This panel also displays each character's status, plus you can view each character's list of Extra Skills by pressing the Square button.

Time to get busy!

The battle is won.

After choosing your bouncer, the character will "react" to being chosen as the leader.

There are also certain sequences in the game where t[...] choice of character will affect the dialogue of the next [...] scene. Thus, the character you choose will change how[...] the story progresses. You get a better idea of the selected character's personality, background, and rela[...] tion to the other characters in the game.

Dominique prefers to go with Sion...

...she feels okay going with Volt...

...but she will complain about being stuck with Kou!

In some instances, character choice will [...] affect the next several Events or even th[...] outcome of the entire game. There are [...] several paths to take in The Bouncer, an[...] several different endings and epilogues t[...] view. Therefore, the game can be a diffe[...] ent experience each time you play. This [...] guide will help you experience every diffe[...] ent ending, while giving away as little of [...] the story as possible.

BATTLES

Battles begin with the player selecting one of the three bouncers to serve as the "leader" of the team. The leader is the character who the playe[...] controls during the fight. The other two characters will fight under the control of the CPU, and will assist the leader in subduing the enemies.

The leader's life meter is displayed in the upper-left corner of the screen, while the life meter of the enemy you're fighting is displayed in the upp[...] right corner of the gameplay screen. The colored dots indicate how many enemies are in the vicinity during the battle. The color of the dot indi[...] cates the status of the enemy. The following summarizes those statuses: Green=Healthy; Yellow=Waning health; Red=Enemy close to being KO'[...] (knocked out).

FIGHTING MOVES

Unlike most action games, characters in The Bouncer are capable of executing both simple and complex combination moves at the touch of a single button. Utilizing the pressure-sensitive technology in the DUALSHOCK™ 2 analog controller for the PlayStation 2, the characters can perform different moves depending on how hard or how lightly you tap the attack buttons. When used in conjunction with analog stick movements and multiple taps, bouncers can perform many different moves by skillfully using a combination of button commands. Even combo moves involving multiple hits are executed with one stroke of a button!

One of Sion's Low attacks kicks the enemy in the leg...

For example, Sion Barzahd has four Low attacks at the start of the game. Here's the breakdown:

- ◎ **MOVE #1:** If you tap the X button lightly (I), he will perform a simple low kick.
- ◎ **MOVE #2:** If you firmly press the X button (L), he will sweep an opponent's feet out from under them.
- ◎ **MOVE #3:** If you tap the X button lightly, and then firmly in succession (I,L), Sion will kick an enemy in the leg and then execute the floor sweep in a *combination attack* that causes more damage.
- ◎ **MOVE #4:** If you are running toward an enemy and press the directional button while tapping X lightly, Sion will slide across the floor into the enemy, knocking them down.

...while a firm button press knocks them flat!

That's 4 whole moves and you haven't even purchased an Extra Skill!

If you are having trouble executing alternate moves with the same button, it seems helpful to press and hold the ES button (L1). For example, if you haven't yet purchased an Extra Skill that uses the Low attack button, then you can press ES + L, and there is a good chance that the bouncer will perform the light-tap move. However, once you purchase an Extra Skill that utilizes the Low attack button, then this bit of advice will no longer work.

You can purchase **Extra Skills** by spending the Bouncer Points you accumulate during the fight. Once you acquire Extra Skills, press and hold the ES button (L1) and press the appropriate button on your controller to execute the move. Using the ES button is kind of like using a "Shift" key, switching the character over to special attack mode for as long as you hold it.

GUARD AND DEFENSE

Mikado's soldiers aren't punching bags; they're not just going to stand there and let you dish it out. Unless your character's Guard is up, the enemy will knock you on your backside just as easily as you do to them!

When an enemy attacks, press the Guard button (R1) to raise the character's defense. The enemy's attack, whether it is a High, Low, Middle, or Jump attack, will be deflected. There's no need to choose an upper or lower guard—you will automatically guard against an enemy's attack. However, the bouncers can only guard against attacks from the front. Attacks from the side or the rear will still hit you, so position your character accordingly in battle. Don't let the enemy get behind you!

Guard will protect you from several blows and even combination attacks, but it doesn't last forever. Your guard is dependent upon your Defense parameter, and each time you guard against an attack, your Defense meter drops a bit. You can check your Defense value from the Pause menu, under Status. When it depletes to zero, you will be unable to guard anymore until the next battle. One indication that your Defense value is decreasing is that the guarding effect gets smaller and the color changes. Also, your character will lower his guarding stance. As is the case with Life, you only get one full Defense meter for each battle. Be especially careful during long battle segments in which your character's condition carries from one fight to the next.

Sion's Defense is obviously low, because he's lowered his guard.

THROW

You can use throwing moves to break an enemy's guard. Throws are Extra Skills, so you can only learn them by spending BP.

The enemy attempts to avoid an attack.

The bouncer picks up the enemy and hurls him!

CHAIN BONUS

When the leader is successful at knocking out an enemy, the number of Bouncer Points gained is momentarily displayed onscreen to the left. If the leader can KO another enemy before the previous score disappears from the screen, then a "Chain Bonus" is achieved.

By performing a Chain Bonus, you can get double, triple, or even quadruple the amount of BP! You can also achieve additional bonus scores by knocking out every enemy yourself.

Sion takes out the trash and scores.

Another swift take-down scores a Chain Bonus!

BOUNCER POINT EXCHANGE

After you've KO'd all the enemies, the battle ends. Bouncer Points for the battle are then tallied and award ed ONLY to the leader. The player then has the option of exchanging Bouncer Points for improvements to the character's Life, Power, and Defense meters. The player can also purchase "Extra Skills," or combat moves that are unique to that particular character. These are special, more intense moves triggered durin battle by pressing attack buttons in combination with the L1, or ES (Extra Skills), button.

CHARACTER RANK

After Bouncer Points have been exchanged, the bouncer may experience an increase in Rank. **Rank will not increase unless you spend BP.** Rank is a reflection of the status of the character, including their Life, Power, and Defense. Extra Skills possessed by a character also determine a bouncer's Rank. But as the Rank of the bouncers increases, so does the Rank of the enemies you face. As a result, enemies will also have higher status meters and more Extra Skills of their own. Refer to the "Enemy Strength Distribution Charts" in each of the Battle Strategies in the **Story Mode** section for more details.

RANKING CHART FOR BOUNCERS	
Bouncer Rank	**BP Consumption**
G-F	1000
F-E	2500
E-D	4700
D-C	7400
C-B	11100
B-A	16100
A-S	23400

OVERALL GAME RANK

Enemy and Boss enemy status and Extra Skills improve as the player's overall "Game Rank" increases. This ranking is determined by the total amount of BP consumption among all three bouncers in Story Mode.

For example, the highest Rank an individual bouncer can achieve is S (Superior). Let's say that by whatever methods, you are able to perfect one of your characters at S Rank, but the other two are only at Rank F and G. Between all three characters, you have only consumed 24900 BP. According to the table that follows, your overall Game Rank is C. When you fight Echidna and the two Security Guards on the MSD Cargo Train, you can use the "Enemy Strength Distribution Chart" presented in the **Story Mode** battle strategy for Battle 6 to determine that she will be Rank C, and the Security Guards will be at Ranks D and C. Then using "Echidna's Status and Skills Chart," you can determine her Life, Power and Defense points, the amount of BP you receive for defeating her, and the Extra Skills she will use in battle. In addition, Echidna will possess the same status and Extra Skills in Versus and Survival Modes.

GAME RANK CHART	
Game Rank	**BP Consumption**
G-F	2400
F-E	6000
E-D	11280
D-C	17760
C-B	26640
B-A	38640
A-S	56160

To sum things up, you can extract from all this information that your Rank S character will have no problem defeating all three enemies, while your Rank G and Rank F characters will be lucky to survive the battle!

THE TRINITY RUSH ATTACK

The Trinity Rush attack is a powerful, three-character combo attack that you can only use in Story Mode. You can only perform this move after one of the two CPU-controlled bouncers gives an audio signal during battle (a whistle or a one-line verbal command).

Once the signal is given, the player can activate the Trinity Rush attack by pressing the "Gesture" button (R2 by default). If the player does not press the "Gesture" button in time, the moment in which the Trinity Rush can be triggered will be missed. The player must then wait until the next audio signal is given. If one of the bouncers gets KO'd, you cannot trigger the Trinity Rush attack.

During the Trinity Rush attack, the three bouncers may appear to be beating up on only one enemy, but this attack actually damages **all** enemies and knocks them to the ground. This move is especially effective when you are surrounded. The moves performed during the Trinity Rush depend upon who the leader is, since that character will finish off the attack with their own special contribution to the move. Try it out with different characters and stages.

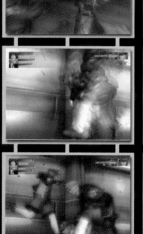

Sion finishes the Trinity Rush.

Volt finishes the Trinity Rush.

Kou finishes the Trinity Rush.

GAME OVER

If the leader gets KO'd by an enemy during battle, the game ends and the player is returned to the Title screen. The player must then reload the last save game and continue from the end of the previous battle.

HIDDEN CHARACTERS

As you progress through Story Mode, you will unlock hidden characters for use in Versus and Survival Mode, complete with their own special moves and fighting style. You can also unlock additional battle arenas as you proceed further into the game.

There are 15 total characters in the game. Most are easily unlocked by completing Story Mode, but some are secret characters that require you to follow certain story paths to unlock. To make all the characters available, refer to the **Unlockable Characters** section in this book. It covers complete bios and move lists for each playable fighter.

LAYOUT SETUP

Now that you understand what the game is like, you need to know how to use this guide to make the most of the experience.

To clear the adventure you will need a good amount of strategy and savvy for each and every battle, and that's exactly what is provided in this guide.

In the **Story Mode** chapter, there's a section for each character along with complete moves lists, detailed tactics for each battle, and tips for the best ways to improve each character as the story progresses. We've decided to make the book "character-based" so that you can get an idea of the best way to train your bouncers, no matter how you play the game.

Although each "Battle Strategy" section follows one character's progress as though he were the only character being used to play the game, that's not necessarily the only way to experience The Bouncer. We want to give you a complete strategy for beating the game, but we don't want to limit you to one character's strategy, and we don't want to spoil the story for you. Yet we want this guide to be an easy-to-reference expert source for the game.

Naturally, we suggest that you attempt to play the game yourself first, without the use of this guide. That way, when you get stuck or face a battle you can't win, you'll have a good understanding of the game, and you'll be able to use the detailed Table of Contents to flip directly to the page describing the event or battle where you are stuck, no matter which bouncer you are playing at any given point of the game.

WARNING: THE THIRD-GAME CHALLENGE

To unlock all of the characters, you must replay the Extra Game of the Story Mode using the same memory card saved game to explore the various pathways and see all the various endings as described in the "Secrets" section of the **Story Mode** section. There is one hidden character that can only be unlocked if you clear the game three times. This third game is where you might experience some difficulty…

As your bouncers become better fighters and attain greater Rank, so do your enemies. The Story Mode Appendix contains "Enemy Strength Distribution Charts" indicating what Rank your enemies will be as compared to your overall Game Rank. For example, the first time you fight Echidna, you are at G Game Rank, so she is Rank G. When you defeat her, she is unlocked in Versus and Survival Modes at G Rank. The second time you fight her in the game, you have consumed a lot more BP and are now probably at Game Rank F. Therefore, Echidna is now also Rank F and is a little harder to defeat the second time. If you manage to outmaneuver her again, her Rank in Versus and Survival Modes is increased to F. This "Ranking Up" of all your regular and hidden characters at the same time makes Versus Mode more interesting to play with your friends, and makes Survival Mode easier. But, oh yes, there is a *catch* to this…

The more you replay The Bouncer, the more difficult it becomes. So if you found your first game unchallenging, don't be disappointed. The enemies will be much more worthy of your fighting abilities in subsequent games. However, near the end of your third game, you should notice that the last few Bosses become *much* more difficult. And then comes the teeth-clencher. Normally, defeating the final Boss requires that you outlast your opponent for two rounds. At the end of a third game, the bouncer you choose to fight the final Boss must be capable of surviving a third *extra bonus round* with this master fighter! Since the final Boss is nearly impossible to defeat in two rounds even at a lower Rank in a first or second game, you will soon realize that surviving this man's attacks for three rounds is something that only a player of some talent can manage. However, if you want to unlock all the hidden characters, it is *absolutely* required that you win this battle.

Whichever method you use to play your first three games to get your three bouncers in shape for the final challenge, there is one simple strategy to keep in mind the whole time that will help you win the final, legendary confrontation: *You must have a delicate balance between improving character status and acquiring Extra Skills!* Repeat this mantra to yourself over and over again as you advance through your replay games.

FEAR NOT!

We're not telling you all this to make you worried about that final three-round confrontation. We've figured out a three-game strategy to defeat that mean old bad guy every time. Even novice players will be able to take him down in style. For more information, turn to the "Secrets" section of the **Story Mode**.

GENERAL NOTES

This section contains a few abbreviations you will see throughout the guide, both in the moves lists and in the battle strategies.

Remember that the PlayStation 2 DUALSHOCK™ 2 analog controller is pressure-sensitive and responds differently in The Bouncer depending on whether you press the control buttons lightly or hard. You cannot get through the game with precision by being a button-masher!

DEFINITIONS

Name	What It Means
Light Attack	Lightly tap the attack button.
Strong Attack	Firmly press the attack button.
Command	Button command needed to execute the fighting move or Extra Skill.
Base Damage	Minimal amount of damage the fighting move or Extra Skill will incur.

LEGEND

Term	Explanation
Direction	Press analog stick or Directional buttons in any direction
h	Light High attack
H	Strong High attack
m	Light Middle attack
M	Strong Middle attack
l	Light Low attack
L	Strong Low attack
j	Light Jump attack
J	Strong Jump attack
(x#)	Press attack button(s) x amount of times
,	Press the 1st button, then the 2nd in quick succession
+	Press both buttons at same time
ES	Extra Skill

STORY INTRODUCTION

Life is difficult, and only the strong survive in the City of Edge. From the rough and tumble bars of Dog Street, you can see the Mikado Building, the headquarters of the multinational Mikado Group Corporation. You can expect to find lots of bouncers in the bars in this part of town. Sion, Kou, and Volt are bouncers who defend their bar, FATE, from any hooligan who tries to invade their territory. Dominique, a young girl found by Sion lying in the middle of town, eventually becomes a mascot for the bar, though nobody really knows where she comes from.

*Mikado Group CEO
Dauragon C. Mikado*

THE MIKADO GROUP CORPORATION

The Mikado Corporation's activities often make headlines. Everyone's attention is often focused on the premier high-technology company. The Mikado Corporation is a massive conglomerate that takes advantage of its advanced technology to expand on space energy research.

The previous head of the Mikado Corporation pushed for a more progressive business style that advocated harmony between the community and the environment. His successor, Dauragon C. Mikado, has announced publicly that he intends to follow through with the same business policy. As the end result, the Space Solar Power Generation Project has been developed.

The City of Edge is adjacent to and shares a close relation with Mikado Aqua City (M.A.C.), an artificial island owned by the corporation located just offshore. This is where Mikado's massive headquarters is housed. Recreational facilities, including a shopping mall and an amusement park, are located on the island as well.

Among the employees of Mikado Corporation, the blue-collar workers reside in the City of Edge, while the white-collar workers reside in Mikado Aqua City.

The Mikado Corporation represents the pinnacle of community bonding and leadership. The technology giant gives back to the citizens in the form of welfare programs and donations to charitable organizations. Mikado sponsors many local sports teams; the Mikado Football Club has won the corporate all-star tournament for three consecutive seasons. It would be difficult to measure the Mikado Corporation's massive contributions to the community.

Mikado has announced that it will soon begin its space development operations with the launch of a shuttle from the Mikado Building's launch facilities.

THE MIKADO BUILDING

The Mikado Building, headquarters and symbol of the Mikado Group, was built to carry out large-scale space development operations. Huge amounts of money are invested in building this massive structure and also in the space project it houses. The building has three towers, each with its own function. One of these towers houses the space shuttle launching facilities. Supported between the three towers lies a "Hanging Garden," with artificial forests and recreational facilities.

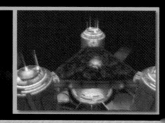

The towers are about 300 meters tall and 100 meters wide. Each of the three towers is named after three sacred items. The main building, 70 stories high, is Kagami Tower and contains the shopping center facility. The space shuttle construction facility is Tsurugi Tower, and most of the rockets are launched from here. The Space Operation building is the Magatama Tower. What transpires in this building is something of a mystery, since only authorized personnel are allowed inside.

In the basement level, a dedicated train station services tens of thousands of visitors and employees daily. With a shopping arcade and entertainment facilities, the Mikado Building functions not only as a simple office building, but as a multi-function structure for the next age.

SPACE SOLAR POWER GENERATION PROJECT

The *Daily COE* (City of Edge) newspaper reports Mikado's business strategy. The paper has strong ties to Mikado and never openly criticizes the company's practices. The paper has been instrumental in gathering public and financial support for the Space Solar Power Generation Project.

Following Mikado's lead, high-tech companies worldwide join the Space Solar Power Generation Project. The following outline is included within the business strategy that CEO Dauragon C. Mikado publicly announced beforehand:

"MIKADO will launch a satellite that converts sunlight into microwave energy beams. The satellite will be controlled from Earth and will collect sunlight, sending a microwave beam to a retrieval facility. The collected microwave beam will be converted into energy, which will then be provided to the rest of the world via a global power conduit. Though there have been previous efforts to use sunlight as an alternate energy source to petroleum and nuclear energy, MIKADO's technology makes it possible to amplify the trace quantities of solar energy for worldwide use."

But as journalists point out, sending powerful beams to the surface of the Earth may have adverse effects on humans and livestock. In addition, due to the price of this new energy, which is assumed to be very high, there is a question as to how many countries will be willing to purchase it. However, since critics have no hard evidence behind their claims, the Mikado Corporation has no intention of changing its position on the matter.

SPACE SHUTTLE GALEOS

The gigantic space shuttle Galeos, made possible through the Mikado Group's great financial power and technology, is not only capable of flying within the atmosphere, it can also fly in space. The gigantic shuttle's length is approximately 360 feet long, with a wingspan of approximately 460 feet. Amazingly, the numerous booster rockets attached to its aft section enable the shuttle to fly into space without the aid of another rocket to help it escape the Earth's gravitational pull.

Because this shuttle was built within the Magatama Tower of the Mikado Building (unauthorized personnel prohibited), no one outside of Mikado knows that it even exists. There are machine guns attached to the outer hull, suggesting that Mikado has intentions other than a space development program, despite previous announcements to the public.

THINGS HAVE BEEN A LITTLE SLOW, LATELY. AND THEN...

For a while, everything is peaceful and quiet. Not even the regular drunks, who sometimes get a little punchy, want to tumble with the three protectors of the FATE bar these days.

Only one bouncer is needed to stand at the door anymore, and Sion has developed a habit of napping upstairs while off duty. But suddenly Dominique is kidnapped by Mikado's Special Forces. What is Mikado up to? What is Dominique's secret? Can Sion and the other bouncers save her? Coming so soon after the recent space shuttle launch by Mikado, could the kidnapping of Dominique be related?

The longest night in the lives of these bouncers is about to begin!

STORY MODE

As explained in the Introduction of this guide, you can choose to fight as one of three bouncers before any given battle. The story perspective switches to that of the bouncer you choose, until you choose a different bouncer. You can play the game with a mix of the three, or you can use one bouncer to play the whole game and soak in their perspective on the events of Story Mode. There are also decisions to make about which bouncer will take the forefront in certain long segments of the game.

This chapter aims to give you all the battle strategy you need to win the game, without ruining the story or showing off too many of the impressive visuals. Thus, only the battles are discussed herein. If we provided a lot of notes on how your choice of bouncers in specific fights affected the events thereafter, then we would spoil the story of the game. To avoid this, we've broken down the Story Mode chapter into sections for each bouncer. So, you get the strategy you need for the bouncer you are trying to use in any given battle, without ruining the rest of the game.

DON'T FORGET...
We should remind you that following only one bouncer's course through the game isn't the only way to go...

SION

Age **19**

Height **5'9"**

Fighting Style **A personalized style of both Kenpo and Street-fighting**

SION BARZAHD

Sion is the youngest bouncer at a bar called FATE. From an early age, he trained in the martial arts under his old-school master, Wong Leung. During that time, Sion met a beautiful young woman and developed a close relationship with her. The world was a beautiful place for many, many years…

Then one day, Master Wong disappeared inexplicably. A year later, his girlfriend got a job at Mikado. Suddenly, an accident killed the only °person he had ever loved. Sion was alone again.

Suffering from severe self-destructive desires, Sion began lashing out at total strangers even on the street. Looking for someone who could defeat him, he eventually bumped into the toughest bouncer on Dog Street. His skills weren't enough to take on the giant, but Sion managed to impress the boss and land a job. He's been working at FATE ever since.

Sion isn't much of a talker and his fellow bouncers really don't know much about him. But recently, there's been a change. Sion found a young woman named Dominique on the street, homeless and alone as he once was. Dominique's bright and warm heart is beginning to open him up again.

Silver accessories are his trademark and Sion loves the DOG STREET brand.

FINAL FANTASY VIII REFERENCE?

This can't be confirmed, but the hound in the FATE Bar logo on the back of Sion's DOG STREET jacket bears a close resemblance to Rinoa's dog, Angelo, from Squaresoft's smash hit, FINAL FANTASY VIII. We've placed screenshots side-by-side here, so compare and decide for yourself. Makes sense, considering the appearance of the cactuar on Volt's jacket, which is a recurring enemy in the FINAL FANTASY series.

SION'S MOVES LIST

Type	Name	Command	Base Damage
Jump	Somersault Heel Drop	j	18
Jump	Cyclone Kick	J	15
Jump	Backflip Kick	j,J	20
Jump	Jumping Spin Kick	Direction + j	13
Jump	Mid-Air Double Kick	Direction + j (x2)	16
High	Jab	h	8
High	One-Two Punch	h,h	8
High	Combo Side Kick	h,h,h	17
High	Roundhouse	H	17
High	Corkscrew Punch	h,H	22
High	Right Dashing Side Kick	Direction + h	14
Middle	Forward Kick	m	8
Middle	Uppercut	M	12
Middle	Double Uppercut	M,m	15
Middle	Double Kick	m,M	11
Middle	Triple Kick	m,M,m	15
Middle	Left Dashing Side Kick	Direction + m	17
Low	Low Kick	l	7
Low	Back Sweep	L	15
Low	Critical Sweep	l,L	18
Low	Sliding Kick	Direction + l	12
ES1	Buster Throw	ES + h	22
ES2	Torpedo Kick	ES + m	19
ES3	Ground Sweep*	ES + l	20
	2nd hit	ES + l (x2)	20
	3rd hit	ES + l (x3)	22
	4th hit	ES + l (x4)	23
	5th hit	ES + l (x5)	24
ES4	Floating Mine	ES + j	21
ES5	Tornado Uppercut	ES + h + j	26
ES6	Double Knuckle	ES + m + l	28
ES7	Hurricane Blitz	ES + j + l	18-32

*This move can be repeated by continuously pressing the low-attack button.

SION'S STATUS UPGRADE BP COSTS

Status Raise	Life	Power	Defense
1-2	200	200	200
2-3	300	300	300
3-4	400	400	400
4-5	500	500	500
5-6	700	700	700
6-7	1000	1000	1000
7-8	1500	1500	1500

SION'S EXTRA SKILLS BP COSTS

Extra Skill	Cost
Buster Throw	400
Torpedo Kick	600
Ground Sweep	1000
Floating Mine	1200
Tornado Uppercut	1600
Double Knuckle	2000
Hurricane Blitz	2800

SION'S STATUS LEVELS

Status	Lv1	Lv2	Lv3	Lv4	Lv5	Lv6	Lv7	Lv8
Life	80	97	115	133	151	169	187	205
Power	55	75	96	117	137	158	179	200
Defense	55	75	95	115	135	155	175	195

BATTLE STRATEGIES

BATTLE 1
"Fate" Bar

Things are slow at the bar.

Dominique gives Sion a present.

Trouble breaks out.

"Dominique!"

This first battle strategy serves as a general introduction to the art of playing as Sion Barzahd. You can apply some strategies and tips that are discussed in this section to **all** of Sion's fights. Other hints are more specific to this encounter.

A quick study of Sion's list of combat moves shows that most of Sion's more powerful combination moves are executed or begun with a light tap on the attack buttons. To utilize the full range of Sion's moves at the beginning of the game, you must acquaint yourself with the difference between a "light tap" and a "heavy tap."

LIGHT BUTTON TAP VS. HEAVY BUTTON TAP

To determine what a "light tap" is as opposed to a "heavy tap," check out the Sensitivity Configuration in the Options menu. Before starting a game, enter the Options menu and select "Controller Settings." Scroll down to the Sensitivity controls for your controller. Leave the sensitivity at Medium; it truly is the most flexible setting. Press the Square button and the meter will measure the strength of your press. A "light tap" fills less than half the meter, and a "heavy tap" is any press that registers above half, no matter how quick.

The first battle pits your three bouncers against five Mikado Special Forces (MSF) soldiers. Since the enemies are all quite a bit higher in Rank here, Sion may get KO'd during this first battle. Don't worry if he does, because this is the one time where the game continues instead of ending if you get knocked out.

Sion starts the game with incredibly weak Power and low Defense and Life meters. Taking out all five enemies on your own in this first battle is quite difficult. As the enemy numbers dwindle, you can aid your fellow bouncers and double-team the remaining stragglers.

Positioning is the key. Throughout all of your battles, it is possible to lose sight of your character. If this occurs, you are bound to take some hits. Move Sion to the forefront of the fighting area, and keep him where he is most visible. Always begin a battle by circling the enemy group until you find one on the outskirts near the forefront, then fight your way inward. Don't pursue enemies that flee or back up into a crowd. A good strategy is to always make the enemy that is **in front of you** the top priority, and do everything to stay out of the middle, where enemies can often attack you from behind.

e MSF have an evasive backflip that makes them tough to attack. Use powerful moves and
mbos that propel Sion toward the enemy, such as the Somersault Heel Drop (j) and the Combo Side
ck (h,h,h). If a MSF fighter performs a Double Back Flip and evades you completely, then use the Sliding
ck (Direction + l) to close the distance. Otherwise, run toward evasive enemies and raise your Guard.

Enemies are positioned on the top and bottom levels of this area. So after you KO a few of the MSF, you can help your buddies finish up or run downstairs on your own to engage the remaining MSF on the ground floor.

Although the Cyclone Kick (J) is great at knocking down two or more enemies at close range, the MSF tend to crouch so low that it rarely works.

"HERE GOES!"

Since there are a lot of enemies in such confined quarters, try using a Trinity Rush attack during this first battle. Just listen for Volt to say "You ready?" and then press the R2 button to set it off immediately. Although it looks like the trio teams up on one foe, actually **all** opponents are damaged in the attack. This makes it much easier to KO more enemies yourself and rake in the BP.

Power Up!

hether you remain conscious or not through your first battle, the first BP Exchange screen appears after this
ht. Since the MSF rank pretty well against you, you should receive 41 or 50 points for each enemy you take down.

u will receive Bonus Points after the battle dependent upon your overall Game Rank. Since you start off at
nk G, you will receive 100 points. Bonus Points received for battles will increase as your Game Rank improves.

changing BP for status improvement is generally more important than purchasing Extra Skills. Begin by
creasing your Power level for 200 BP, so that your attacks and combos have more punch.

you can KO enemies more quickly, then you can fight more enemies, score more points, and level up your
her stats even more quickly. Life should be the next best thing you improve, followed by Defense.

BATTLE 2
Central Square

EVENT SEQUENCE

Dominique is kidnapped.

Kou gets some information.

The trio head for the MSD Cargo Train.

Interceptors appear outside the Station.

It's Raining MSF...

In the first battle, your character began in an optimum position on the outside of the fighting area, and the enemies were surrounded. This time it's the other way around, so you must first concentrate on positioning Sion safely out of harm's way. The MSF are much lower in Rank this time and much easier to fight.

The same fighting tactics used in the last fight still apply and are even more effective here. Focus on using Sion's more damaging combination moves, and use the Somersault Heel Drop (j) and Combo Side Kick (h,h,h) attacks to stay close to evasive MSFs.

Getting double-teamed is a greater possibility in this fight. But due to the low Rank of the MSF soldiers, you don't have much to worry about. Knock down one enemy, and then move Sion to face the other enemy waiting patiently nearby.

Most of the battle will probably occur in the lower courtyard area, but it is possible to lead enemies to the upper area. If you can't find any enemies and the fight is still ongoing, rest assured that your bouncer buddies have led the enemies upstairs.

BATTLE 3
Central Station

EVENT SEQUENCE

Sion spots a mysterious black panther.

The station is heavily guarded.

The bouncers are spotted!

Economy Class, Please

Finally, a battle where even novice players can truly shine! Security Guards are the lowest order on the Mikado food chain and the easiest to defeat. Because they remain mostly upright, they are susceptible to the full range of your combat moves, including the Jumping Spin Kick (Direction + j) and Sion's Roundhouse (H). However, using combination moves such as Triple Kick (m,M,m) and the Corkscrew Punch (h,H) will increase your chances of knocking out all three Guards yourself.

BATTLE 4
Central Station (Timed)

EVENT SEQUENCE

The MSD Cargo Train finishes loading.

Security Guards notice your handiwork.

Kou explains the time limit.

A Frenzied Fight

s Kou mentions, there is a certain time limit to this battle. No
mer is displayed on-screen, and the whistle doesn't sound until
he events following the battle. The fight will simply end after **45
econds!** If you KO all the enemies on-screen before that, then
he heroes get onboard the train. If not, then Sion misses the
rain and struggles to catch up. It's almost worth it not to defeat
ll the enemies here, because the cut-scene becomes a little
ore exciting!

t the start of the fight, the Security Guards will meet your team near a lamppost. Steer Sion to the forefront of the cluster, and pick on a guy at the
dge. If you knock him down before their cluster spreads out, all the enemies will fall like dominoes! This is a great way to damage all foes at once.

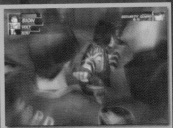

lso, it seems feasible to use the Trinity Rush attack during this timed struggle. We've triggered the
ttack at least once or twice during the battle and still had time to take out all the enemies with Sion!

BATTLE 5
MSD Cargo Train

EVENT SEQUENCE

he bouncers
ow away on
the train.

Echidna dispatches her troops.

The bouncers climb into battle.

Protectors of the Cargo Train

The character you choose to fight in this situation must duke it out for two rounds with two sets of three Security Guards. But if you can KO a lot of enemies, you can increase Sion's status and maybe even Rank Up. That would be a good thing, considering that the first Boss fight is coming up!

Beware of getting knocked down in close quarters. If a bouncer (or foe) gets knocked down, he may take out 3-4 unwary characters with him. To avoid this, make sure you block.

Gradually make your way around the enemies, so that you and your fellow bouncers surround them. This means that the Guards will have their unprotected backs to each other, and you may be able to knock them all down when you take down one.

BATTLE 6
Echidna (Boss) & Security Guards (2)

BOSS

ECHIDNA'S STATUS CHART

Status	Rank							
	G	F	E	D	C	B	A	S
Life	110	122	135	148	161	174	187	200
Power	80	93	107	120	134	147	161	175
Defense	90	106	122	139	155	172	188	205
BP	120	160	200	240	280	320	360	480

BOSS

ECHIDNA'S EXTRA SKILLS

ES	Rank							
	G	F	E	D	C	B	A	S
Missile Kick	*	*	*	*	*	*	*	*
Cyclone Drive	-	*	*	*	*	*	*	*
Dead-End Carnival	-	-	*	*	*	*	*	*
Double Slap	-	-	-	*	*	*	*	*
Ambush Strike	-	-	-	-	*	*	*	*

The Woman Warrior

After dusting off most of the train's security, the bouncers are confronted by the leader of the pack on top of the speeding train. Needless to say, the two Security Guards accompanying Echidna are not much of a threat. But don't underestimate Echidna; her unique fighting style enables her to compensate for her petite size!

When the battle commences, raise your bouncer's Guard to avoid Echidna's initial attack. When the attack finishes, immediately counter with a Critical Sweep (I,L). Get used to performing this combination move and other Low attacks to counter Echidna's low crouch.

She is especially susceptible to Low attacks, but since Sion's Low attacks are not terribly powerful, this battle could take some time. Be prepared to block at all times; make it a priority over attacking. It's possible to perform the Trinity Rush attack on Echidna, so use it as many times as possible.

efeating Echidna ends the battle immediately, even if the Security uards are still standing. Don't worry about the Guards unless one ets right in front of or behind you. Of course, it adds to your total oints if you can defeat them.

CARD KEY EVENT

After clearing the train of enemies, an attack by a mysterious fighter-plane disables the brakes. The train will crash into the station and the rocket fuel tanks will detonate if the Card Key is not found in time. If Sion is selected to find the Card Key, he has 20 seconds to find it. Again, the time isn't displayed on-screen, so search quickly.

*There are three boxes in the cab: one to the left, one to the right, and one on the floor by the doorway. Simply move Sion to any box and he will automatically search it. The Card Key is always inside the **last** box you search. If the Card Key is found in time, the rocket fuel tanks will be disengaged and the train will simply crash into the station.*

*However, if the tanks are **not** released in time, the train will detonate upon impact and sea water will begin flooding the station. This affects the next long battle, causing emergency shutters to close. The Game Over screen will appear if you get caught behind a shutter. The enemies encountered are also tougher, as explained in the next section, Battle 7.*

BATTLE 7
Emergency Passage (Normal Scenario)

EVENT SEQUENCE

The rocket fuel tanks are released.

The bouncers escape the train.

Security Guards block the corridors.

A Minimum of Resistance

Getting through the emergency corridors is simple if you succeed in finding and using the Card Key onboard the MSD Cargo Train. There are four to five enemies on each floor, but only three will attack at the outset. The reinforcements arrive shortly from the other section of the corridor, so it's important to take 'em down quickly.

EMERGENCY PASSAGE (NORMAL)
CARD KEY FOUND IN TIME

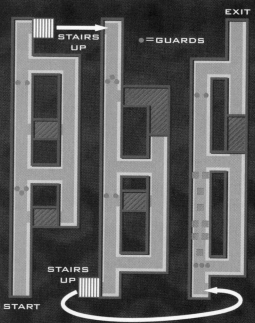

STAIRS UP

● = GUARDS

EXIT

STAIRS UP

START

The guards wearing black vests and listening to headsets are called Security Chiefs, and pose more problems than their simpler underlings. They are quicker to counterattack and more likely to block your attacks. Since you must travel three floors of enemies with only one full Life bar, you must be very cautious against Security Chiefs and use your Guard wisely.

LISTEN FOR HELP!

If you fail to neutralize the first wave of security before your foe's backup arrives, then remember to listen for the signal to trigger the Trinity Rush attack.

After disposing of all the enemies on a floor (check the enemy status bar in the upper-right corner), run to the end of the corridor and up the stairs to the next level. If you get lost, run toward a wall and look for a white arrow directing you to the exit (or refer to the map). Also, you don't need to wait for slower comrades; they will be upstairs when the next round begins. The battle ends when you reach a big door marked "EXIT."

THE RECOMMENDED PATH!

Finding the Card Key and disconnecting the rocket fuel cars from the train in time make the battles in the Emergency Passage much easier. If you don't find the Card Key in time, then you must contend with more difficult enemies in greater numbers, plus you must outrun closing emergency shutters and follow twisting corridors.

BATTLE 7
Emergency Passage
(Closing Shutters Scenario)

EVENT SEQUENCE

The Card Key isn't found in time.

The train destroys the station.

Sea water floods the corridors.

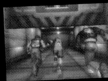
The emergency shutters are closing!

So You Couldn't Find the Card Key...

...or perhaps you *decided not to.* The latter reason is the more likely case. The scenario in the MSD Station is different because of the sea water flooding the area. The emergency shutters begin to close behind you, and several sections of straightaway corridor are already sealed off.

The only real challenge in the first battle is the Security Chief. After disposing of all the enemies, Sion must run under a series of closing shutter doors. This is easily accomplished by using the Analog Stick instead of the Directional button. Continue running forward and around the corner until you catch up to your buddies.

EMERGENCY PASSAGE (ALTERNATE)
CARD KEY NOT FOUND IN TIME

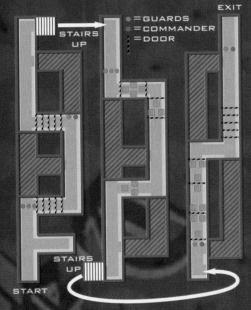

In the next round, two more enemies come charging in from the distance. One is a Commander, an enemy that you only encounter in this alternate scenario. Commanders can be difficult to take down, largely due to their advanced Defense and Power stats. They will also knock you to the ground with a shoulder-butt if given the opportunity.

To dispose of Commanders, use your team of bouncers. Take out any minor enemies first (like the lowly Security Guards), and then surround the Commander in a triangle-shaped formation. This prevents the Commander from blocking all attacks.

You must then outrun more closing shutters in another corridor. Turn Sion to his right and continue down the corridor to the steps (or refer to the map). In this scenario, you must go up two flights of steps and down a short stretch of hallway to reach your buddies.

The battle continues in this manner until you defeat all the enemies on the third floor. Be more cautious when facing the Commanders and Security Chiefs, and you should rack up a lot of Bouncer Points. Use them to improve Sion's Defense and Life status.

BATTLE 8
Air-Carrier

EVENT SEQUENCE

Volt opens the Emergency Exit doors.

Air-Carriers are searching the area.

The bouncers hitch a ride.

Hijacking!!!

Landing on a Mikado Air-Carrier may or may not be Sion's best idea. Carrier Soldiers are tough commandos in the organization's ranks, and shouldn't be taken lightly. Your group is half-surrounded at the beginning of the match. Raising your Guard should prevent a quick knockdown by your foes.

This is one of the few scraps where it's **not** wise to move Sion to the forefront, because you could potentially take a lot of damage along the way. The closest enemy to Sion's starting position is the one in the back left corner. Fight him to prevent him from double-teaming one of your mates, and things should be pretty evenly matched.

When fighting Carrier Soldiers, it's best to keep your Guard up and let the perform one or two moves before retaliating. Carrier Soldiers attack more often and more viciously than previous enemies. Since you're fighting in su close quarters, try to send one of them flying with a move such as the Tri Kick (m,M,m) or the Double Uppercut (M,m). The end result may send you foe flying into his buddies, damaging everyone.

Use a Trinity Rush attack at least once on the Air-Carrier. With the scrolli background and different camera angles, it's a visual feast as well as a sa fying pounding against your enemies.

BATTLE 9
Hanging Garden

EVENT SEQUENCE

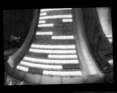

The Air-Carrier flies up the Mikado Building.

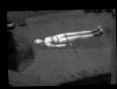

Sion spots Dominique.

Volt crashes the carrier.

Watchdogs are alerted to the heroes' presence.

Rocky Landing

[I]s a wonder the whole Mikado brigade isn't tracking Sion and the others through the Hanging Garden, [co]nsidering how poorly Volt lands the Air-Carrier! But still, the trio is spotted by the Watchdogs known as [J]akilla," and MSF soldiers are dispatched to help the doggies take you out.

[At] the outset of this battle, take out the closest Watchdog with a Sliding Kick (Direction + l) followed by [se]veral Critical Sweep combos (l,L). Although the hounds aren't as dangerous as the MSF, you don't want [to] discount them, either.

You can fight the MSF with the same tactics as in previous battles. Use the Double Uppercut (M,m) or Triple Kick (m,M,m) while they are in front of you. If they perform a backflip, follow them with the Somersault Heel Drop (j) or the Sliding Kick.

BATTLE 10
Mugetsu (Boss) & MSF Soldiers (4)

BOSS

MUGETSU W/MASK STATUS CHART

Status	Rank							
	G	F	E	D	C	B	A	S
Life	110	124	138	152	167	181	195	210
Power	90	105	121	137	152	168	184	200
Defense	70	84	98	112	127	141	155	170
BP	150	200	250	300	350	400	450	600

MUGETSU W/MASK EXTRA SKILLS

ES	Rank							
	G	F	E	D	C	B	A	S
Ren-Getsu	-	-	✳	✳	✳	✳	✳	✳
Gen-Getsu (Hell)	✳	✳	✳	✳	✳	✳	✳	✳
Gen-Getsu (Heaven)	✳	✳	✳	✳	✳	✳	✳	✳
Hi-Getsu	-	-	-	-	✳	✳	✳	✳

The Psycho Man

How does it feel to have your woman taken away from you...?

[As] Mugetsu arrives at the scene, it seems his sanity is decaying at a rapid pace. He fights like a wild [an]imal, taking on the nearest bouncer with reckless abandon. Don't allow Sion to become the center of [M]ugetsu's focus; if this occurs, Mugetsu will repeatedly pound Sion. The battle becomes very hard to [su]rvive if this happens.

Fight the multiple MSF soldiers with the tactics you've used up to this point. Your best moves are the Corkscrew Punch (h,H) and the Backflip Kick (j,J). If they backflip away, use the Somersault Heel Drop (j) or Sliding Kick (Direction + l) to pursue them in an offensive manner.

During the first part of the battle, attack Mugetsu only if he draws near. Unleash a few punches or kicks, something really strong to knock him away, and then focus on the lesser foe. Don't leave an active MSF on your flank, or he and Mugetsu may knock you back and forth until your Life runs out.

Throughout the fight, listen for the audio signal from your teammate and use a Trinity Rush attack whenever possible. As the enemy forces dwindle, your trio can focus their attention on the madman.

Focus on using Middle and High moves, such as the Corkscrew Punch (h,H) and the Triple Kick (m,M,m). Mugetsu resistant to Jump moves (such as the Cyclone Kick and Jumping Spin Kick), but the Mid-Air Double Kick (Direction (x2)) might catch him off-guard, especially with the second hit of the combo.

Low attacks from Sion don't have enough power, plus Mugetsu can easily block them. The most effective Low attac the Sliding Kick (Direction + I). However, you should only use this when Mugetsu is evading with a backflip.

BATTLE 11
Dauragon (Boss) & Black Panther

EVENT SEQUENCE

Sion finds a way inside the dome.

Dauragon says goodbye to Wong.

The villain offers to fight the bouncers one-handed.

I shall add another handicap as well.

BOSS

ONE-ARMED DAURAGON'S STATUS CHART

Status	Rank							
	G	F	E	D	C	B	A	S
Life	120	134	148	162	177	191	205	220
Power	70	88	107	125	144	162	181	200
Defense	70	82	95	108	121	134	147	160
BP	110	146	183	220	256	293	330	440

BOSS

ONE-ARMED DAURAGON'S EXTRA SKILLS

ES	Rank							
	G	F	E	D	C	B	A	S
Whirlwind Kick	*	*	*	*	*	*	*	*
Crescent Moon Slash	*	*	*	*	*	*	*	*
Triple Rave Kick	-	-	-	-	*	*	*	*
Elbow Spear	-	-	*	*	*	*	*	*

BOSS

??? (BLACK PANTHER) STATUS CHART

Status	Rank							
	G	F	E	D	C	B	A	S
Life	100	113	127	140	154	167	181	195
Power	70	84	98	112	127	141	155	170
Defense	90	105	121	137	152	168	184	200
BP	120	160	200	240	280	320	360	480

BATTLE 13
Mikado Building—66F Hall

The Search Party

A large group awaits Sion on the 66th floor. This battle is completely unavoidable and is a must-win in Sion's scenario.

Whatever you do, don't charge in. If you do, a P-101 will join in the battle and make things more difficult. Wait for one or two Security Guards to run at Sion, and then dispose of them with combo moves like the Triple Kick (m,M,m) and Combo Side Kick (h,h,h).

While fighting the humans, a robot may join the fight but the others will most likely stay near the exit. When fighting the Guards, use Jump attacks like the Backflip Kick (j,J), the Cyclone Kick (J) and the Mid-Air Double Kick (Direction + j (x2)). It's likely that if you attack a Guard with jump moves, a P-101 attacking from behind will miss if you are in mid-air.

If the P-101 gets too close, give it a few Low Kicks (l) to back it off. You don't want to focus solely on taking out a robot first, because the Guards will run up and attack from behind.

BATTLE 14
Mikado Building—Data Room

Access Denied

While viewing the information contained in the last file on the computer console, MSF and MSF elite soldiers burst into the room and dismantle the monitor. Because of the narrow confines, focus your attacks on whichever enemy is closer. If you knock one to the floor, wait for him to get back up. *Try not to* engage the other enemy until you have KO'd the first one!

MSF crouch low, which nullifies most Jump attacks and some High moves. Instead, rely on moves like the Double Uppercut (M,m), Triple Kick (m,M,m), and Left Dashing Side Kick (Direction + m). If an enemy backflips away, perform Sion's Somersault Heel Drop (j) or the Sliding Kick (Direction + l) to move in close.

MSF Elites block more often than regular MSF. If you have Sion's Buster Throw (ES + h), you can nullify the strong Guard of an MSF Elite. It should be noted that this move is *NOT* essential to defeating Elites.

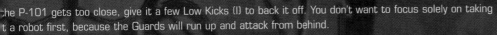

BATTLE 15

Black Panther (Sub-Boss)

??? (BLACK PANTHER) STATUS CHART

Status	Rank							
	G	F	E	D	C	B	A	S
Life	100	113	127	140	154	167	181	195
Power	70	84	98	112	127	141	155	170
Defense	90	105	121	137	152	168	184	200
BP	120	160	200	240	280	320	360	480

??? (BLACK PANTHER) EXTRA SKILLS

Name	Rank							
	G	F	E	D	C	B	A	S
Spinning Rush	*	*	*	*	*	*	*	*
Wild Fang	-	-	-	*	*	*	*	*

Bizarre Confrontation

Sion takes the stairs out of the Data Room and up to the Executive level. Move down the hallway until a cut-scene starts. At this point, Sion is cut off from his goal and trapped with the mysterious Black Panther.

Quickly raise your Guard to deflect the panther's initial charge. Then knock the beast flat with a Back Sweep (L) or a combo Critical Sweep (I,L). Because the creature has a low stance, Sion must rely on mostly Low attacks.

Perform several Low Kicks (I) followed by a Critical Sweep in succession. You can also use the Somersault Heel Drop (j), but there's a chance it may miss. If the panther retreats or circles Sion, catch up to it with the Sliding Kick (Direction + I).

BATTLE 19

Mugetsu (Boss), MSF Soldiers (2), & MSF Elite (2)

BOSS

MUGETSU W/MASK STATUS CHART

Status	Rank							
	G	F	E	D	C	B	A	S
Life	110	124	138	152	167	181	195	210
Power	90	105	121	137	152	168	184	200
Defense	70	84	98	112	127	141	155	170
BP	150	200	250	300	350	400	450	600

BOSS

MUGETSU W/MASK EXTRA SKILLS

ES	Rank							
	G	F	E	D	C	B	A	S
Ren-Getsu	-	-	※	※	※	※	※	※
Gen-Getsu (Hell)	※	※	※	※	※	※	※	※
Gen-Getsu (Heaven)	※	※	※	※	※	※	※	※
Hi-Getsu	-	-	-	-	※	※	※	※

EVENT SEQUENCE

Sion finds Dominique at last.

Mugetsu attacks!

Volt joins the party.

Kou makes a comic entrance.

Some Guys Never Learn...

Seeking vengeance for his past humiliation at your hands, Mugetsu has created a very clever trap for Sion in the Executive Office. Fortunately, this is where Sion's solo scenario ends, at which point he's rejoined by Volt and Kou. However, a tough battle awaits the reunited heroes!

It's best to adopt Mugetsu's roaming-fighting method. Concentrate most of your efforts against the MSF and Elite soldiers at first, using the same tactics as before. Use the Corkscrew Punch (h,H) and the Backflip Kick (j,J) on MSF that come in close range. If they backflip away, use the Somersault Heel Drop (j) or Sliding Kick (Direction + l) to stay close.

Focus on the first enemy that engages Sion, until he gets KO'd or runs away. Move Sion out of the center, so that his back is against a wall. When Mugetsu draws near while you're fighting another foe, execute a move that will knock down your current opponent and then turn your attention to Mugetsu.

31

Use a Trinity Rush attack when you get the chance. It's helpful to dispose of all the MSF and Elite enemies before taming Mugetsu.

When fighting Mugetsu, use Middle and High moves such as the Corkscrew Punch (h,H) and the Triple Kick (m,M,m). The Boss is resistant to Jump moves such as the Cyclone Kick and Jumping Spin Kick, but the Mid-Air Double Kick (Direction + j (x2)) may catch him off-guard, especially with the second hit of the combo.

Sion's Low attacks aren't powerful enough, plus Mugetsu can block them. But don't forget the Sliding Kick (Direction + l); use it when Mugetsu is trying to evade you. The battle ends when Mugetsu is defeated.

BATTLE 20
Rocket Tower 6F to 2F

EVENT SEQUENCE

Dominique is revived.

The Rocket Tower goes on full alert.

The team decides to split up.

The Robot Horde

The bouncer chosen to accompany Dominique through the Rocket Tower must survive a multi-level gauntlet of robot sentinels. Keep in mind the following conditions:

◎ You must complete all levels with only **one** Life bar; no breaks or refills.

◎ Dominique must survive all levels with **one** Life bar; if she doesn't, it's "Game Over."

◎ If Sion's or Dominique's Life meters are near 25% or less, you'd best stop fighting and run directly to the exit.

◎ Against all robots, you should choose single, non-combo moves that you can quickly repeat over and over. Avoid using moves that take a long time to recover from, such as Jump moves or floor sweeps. The robots **will retaliate** in between your attacks if given the chance.

A character with a higher Rank is better suited to take on every robot and enemy in the Rocket Tower. As a beginner at F or E Rank (estimated), pick your battles wisely and skip as many enemies as possible. This section provides some pointers on who to fight, who not to fight, and how to survive.

Your initial fighting decision comes on the first platform. With an LD-15 (big orange robot) in front and one moving in from behind, you must prevent Sion and Dominique from taking damage right from the start. Run over to the side wall and lead Dominique around the platform to the exit stairs.

On the next level down, you'll encounter the gray humanoid robots called MC-07. These robots are much easier to destroy than any other. Use the Combo Side Kick (h,h,h) to push them back, and then fly in close with the Somersault Heel Drop (j). As with most robots, you can interrupt the MC-07's attacks with your own. Since most of this robot's moves are performed up high with its arms, you can interrupt its attacks in mid-motion by performing a simple Low Kick (l).

eware of an incoming LD-15 behind the MC-07; you don't want get surrounded. If the MC-07 gets knocked behind the LD-15, en attack the larger worker droid.

Vhen fighting LD-15s, use short, non-combo moves such as the ppercut (M) or the One-Two Punch (h,h). Continue to use either these moves constantly. This is the best way to outlast the D-15 without taking a lot of damage.

roceed up the stairs to take on another MC-07, and then escend the next set of stairs and run past the next LD-15 to e exit. Only when you are replaying the game with a higher ank should you tangle with the last robot.

fter defeating the lone Security Guard at the bottom of the stairs on the 4th floor, you'll encounter some MC-07s up the stairs. If Sion's Rank is till low, you may want to avoid this fight. Down the stairs, a Security Chief will engage Sion. Keep your Guard up until he attacks, and then etaliate with a powerful move like Backflip Kick (j,J) or the Corkscrew Punch (h,H).

ake the stairs down to Level 3 and move to the left, where two bridge structures connect to the next platform. *Avoid* the LD-15 blocking the ght bridge, and lead Dominique to the place where the MC-07 awaits. You can fight this lone robot, but be aware that another MC-07 and an D-15 are moving in.

Another set of dual bridges will take you to the next platform. You can avoid confrontation with the LD-15 and the MC-07 altogether by crossing on the left-hand bridge. To the left of their position is the stairwell down to the final level.

If you move Sion straight ahead from the bottom of the steps, you'll encounter a lone MC-07 that is easy to take out. Beyond it is the green-colored lift that marks the exit, and this long and tense battle will end once you step off the platform. Advanced bouncers with higher Ranks may want to take out the MC-07 and the LD-15 at the opposite end of this platform before leaving, however, just to get those BP!

BATTLE 21

PD-4 (Boss)

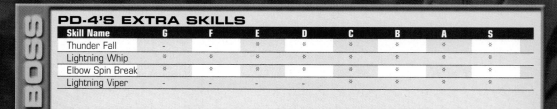

PD-4'S STATUS CHART

Status	Rank							
	G	F	E	D	C	B	A	S
Life	120	134	148	162	177	191	205	220
Power	90	102	115	128	141	154	167	180
Defense	95	107	120	133	146	159	172	185
BP	170	226	283	340	396	453	510	680

PD-4'S EXTRA SKILLS

Skill Name	G	F	E	D	C	B	A	S
Thunder Fall	-	-	※	※	※	※	※	※
Lightning Whip	※	※	※	※	※	※	※	※
Elbow Spin Break	※	※	※	※	※	※	※	※
Lightning Viper	-	-	-	-	※	※	※	※

The Prototype Superweapon

Sion and Dominique run into PD-4 on the lowest level of the Rocket Tower. This evil prototype bionoid craves only death and destruction. While it has been ordered to retrieve Dominique, Volt and Kou arrive to help Sion prevent that from happening. PD-4 doesn't mind the challenge one bit.

Raise Sion's Guard and deflect PD-4's initial attack. Take note that PD-4 uses long, multi-hit combo moves but needs time to recover afterward. Keep your Guard up the whole time it attacks. When the attack ceases, let loose with your own counterattack. Sion's best moves against PD-4 are the Combo Side Kick (h,h,h), the Corkscrew Punch (h,H), the Double Uppercut (M,m), and the Triple Kick (m,M,m).

Attempt to surround the bionoid with your bouncers so that it will have trouble defending itself. Use Sion's most powerful moves and combos; don't waste an opportunity on simple, low-caliber kicks or floor sweeps.

Use a Trinity Rush attack whenever possible. There should be several opportunities, since you'll probably spend most of the fight with your Guard up.

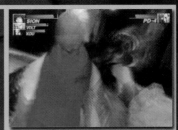

BATTLE 22
Rocket Tower—Basement

EVENT SEQUENCE

Mugetsu takes Dominique to the Galeos.

An enraged Sion pursues Mugetsu.

The LD-X1 debuts.

Toys in the Basement

The black loader robot is slightly stronger and has more Life than the other two. Take out the LD-15s first using quick attacks with short recovery times, such as the One-Two Punch (h,h) or the Double Uppercut (M,m).

It's important to stay close to the loader as you pound away at it, and many of Sion's blows will propel the enemy away. If the distance gets to be too great, it gives the loader a chance to counterstrike. Use Sion's Somersault Heel Drop (j) or the Sliding Kick (Direction + l) to get closer to the loader.

The LD-X1 is a bit nastier, but if all of your bouncers are still in the mix, then triple-teaming it should do the job. Move Sion behind it, and use your Guard if it rears back.

Power Up!

If you've been exchanging your BP for mostly status upgrades throughout the game, then your bouncers should be in good shape for the last four battles. That's good news, because they're all Boss fights!

When your BP and Bonus Points are tallied up this time, treat yourself to one of Sion's moves called the Torpedo Kick, if you haven't done so already. It will help out immensely in the uphill struggle that follows.

BATTLE 23

Echidna (Boss) & LD-X1 Robots (x2)

ECHIDNA'S STATUS CHART

Status	Rank							
	G	F	E	D	C	B	A	S
Life	110	122	135	148	161	174	187	200
Power	80	93	107	120	134	147	161	175
Defense	90	106	122	139	155	172	188	205
BP	120	160	200	240	280	320	360	480

ECHIDNA'S EXTRA SKILLS

ES	Rank							
	G	F	E	D	C	B	A	S
Missile Kick	*	*	*	*	*	*	*	*
Cyclone Drive	-	*	*	*	*	*	*	*
Dead-End Carnival	-	-	*	*	*	*	*	*
Double Slap	-	-	-	*	*	*	*	*
Ambush Strike	-	-	-	-	*	*	*	*

A Woman's Wrath

The red-headed vixen is back! This time, she's learned her lesson and brought along better support. The two LD-X1s are like giant moving walls. They've been programmed to assist Echidna in annihilating everyone.

Raise your Guard immediately to counteract Echidna's Capoeira spinning fighter moves. If not, you'll get knocked down. When she gets up, hit her with a Critical Sweep (I,L) followed by a Somersault Heel Drop (j). When performed correctly, you will knock her to the ground and hit her again while she is down. Immediately face the nearest LD-X1, and continue to fight!

Focus on eliminating a machine by hitting it with easily controllable moves like the Double Uppercut (M,m) and the Corkscrew Punch (h,H).

Because Echidna hovers so close to the ground, rely on moves like the Critical Sweep (I,L) and the Double Uppercut (M,m). That's why we suggested that you have Sion learn the Torpedo Kick (ES + m) after the last battle. It provides another powerful move to use against her. Remember to use a Trinity Rush attack when you hear the signal. When Echidna dives for the floor, press the R1 button to block her attacks!

BATTLE 24
Mugetsu (Boss)

EVENT SEQUENCE

The Galeos launches.

The bouncers grab a ride.

Mugetsu leaps aboard the Air-Carrier!

Hyah hah hah...! I've been waiting for you...

MUGETSU W/O MASK STATUS CHART

Status	Rank							
	G	F	E	D	C	B	A	S
Life	120	134	148	162	177	191	205	220
Power	100	115	131	147	162	178	194	210
Defense	65	79	93	107	122	136	150	165
BP	180	240	300	360	420	480	540	720

MUGETSU W/O MASK EXTRA SKILLS

Name	Rank							
	G	F	E	D	C	B	A	S
Shi-Getsu	-	✳	✳	✳	✳	✳	✳	✳
Fuku-Getsu	-	-	-	-	✳	✳	✳	✳
Ka-Getsu	-	-	✳	✳	✳	✳	✳	✳
Ren-Getsu	✳	✳	✳	✳	✳	✳	✳	✳

Psycho Boy Strikes Back!

Commandeering an Air-Carrier and sneaking onboard the space shuttle Galeos should be a snap for these three Mikado-fighting veterans, right? Wrong! The psychopathic Mugetsu has gone completely mental, and flings himself onto the transport. Without the constraints of caution and reason, you'll find that Mugetsu is a much more lethal opponent this time.

Your first decision is, "Who's going to fly the carrier?" Since this strategy is for Sion to fight, it's obvious that you don't want him piloting the craft.

<tch>... Who's going to pilot this thing?

Raise your Guard and wait for Mugetsu to attack. He will most likely perform a Crazy Drill, where he instantly becomes horizontal and launches like a torpedo. This move requires a second or two for him to recover and regain his battle stance, so take the opportunity to perform a Triple Kick (m,M,m).

When Mugetsu gets back up, try to get him between you and your partner. If he goes after your partner, kick him from the rear. If not, raise your Guard and wait for him to attack again and then perform another combo move such as the Double Uppercut (M,m) or the Corkscrew Punch (h,H).

Since there are only two of you engaged in the battle, you cannot perform a Trinity Rush attack. Also, you don't want to let your partner get KO'd. Taking on Mugetsu in his psychotic state is a little more than you can handle alone.

Beware also of the Ren-Getsu, a move where Mugetsu begins spinning like a top above the ground. When this occurs, keep your Guard up the whole time to avoid taking damage.

Mugetsu doesn't block much but he does attack swiftly and often. If Sion knows the Extra Skill Torpedo Kick, use it to counter Mugetsu's constant barrage of two-handed chops. Sion dives right under the lunatic and kicks him high into the air.

BATTLE 25
Black Panther (Sub-Boss)

BLACK PANTHER'S STATUS CHART

Status	Rank							
	G	F	E	D	C	B	A	S
Life	100	113	127	140	154	167	181	195
Power	70	84	98	112	127	141	155	170
Defense	90	105	121	137	152	168	184	200
BP	120	160	200	240	280	320	360	480

BLACK PANTHER'S EXTRA SKILLS

Name	Rank							
	G	F	E	D	C	B	A	S
Griffin Talons	-	-	*	*	*	*	*	*
Meteor Storm	*	*	*	*	*	*	*	*
Griffin Tail	-	-	-	-	*	*	*	*
Spinning Rush	*	*	*	*	*	*	*	*
Wild Fang	-	-	-	*	*	*	*	*
Shape Shift	*	*	*	*	*	*	*	*

Beautiful Stranger

Onboard the Galeos, the mysterious Black Panther leaps into the path and prevents the bouncers from reaching the control room. Looks like Dauragon's strange pet has an overwhelming need to protect him.

Since the panther is so low to the ground, Low attacks are the key. You can move Sion closer to the beast by executing a Sliding Kick (Direction + I), which should cause some damage. Repeatedly attack the beast with Low Kicks (I) and the Critical Sweep combo (I,L). When the beast growls, prepare to block.

everal times during the battle, the panther shape-shifts into a uman female form. This bizarre woman attacks with sweeping i-chi based movements. After deflecting her attacks, use the ombo Side Kick (h,h,h) to knock her to the ground, or launch r high into the air with the Torpedo Kick (ES + m) (if available).

BATTLE 26

Dauragon II (Boss)

BOSS

BOSS

DAURAGON'S STATUS CHART

Status	Rank							
	G	F	E	D	C	B	A	S
Life	125	140	155	170	185	200	215	230
Power	80	97	114	131	148	165	182	200
Defense	80	94	108	122	137	151	165	180
BP	150	200	250	300	350	400	450	600

DAURAGON'S EXTRA SKILLS

Name	Rank							
	G	F	E	D	C	B	A	S
Whirlwind Kick	※	※	※	※	※	※	※	※
Crescent Moon Slash	※	※	※	※	※	※	※	※
Dragon Claw	-	-	※	※	※	※	※	※
Dragon Blitz	※	※	※	※	※	※	※	※
Wyvern's Sting	-	-	-	-	※	※	※	※

This is your reward for being such a nuisance...!

King of Fighters

So, do you think you're ready to fight Dauragon when he uses *both* hands? We'll see!

ou must fight *two* rounds with the prince of fisticuffs, and you cannot select a different bouncer between rounds. Also, your Life bar will not refill etween battles. This battle will severely drain Sion's Defense meter. Without your ability to block, Dauragon will make quick work of you.

he control room of the Galeos provides ample floor space for sparring, but there are curved areas to the left and right of Dominique's position hat you must be aware of. When using the following strategy, avoid this part of the fighting area.

t the start of the fight, move Sion back a step and then circle the group to the left. Typically, Dauragon begins circling to the left as well, and if you et behind him you suddenly have him surrounded! Keep your Guard up until he turns his back, and then perform a fierce combo attack to his rear.

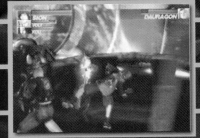

Stay on the move and then settle back into Guard stance to protect Sion. You want to keep Dauragon surrounded constantly by the bouncers. Volt and Kou will usually take up positions in a triangular shape as long as you move around Dauragon. They will follow your lead as well.

With bouncers on all sides, Dauragon will attack and defend in all different directions, and even performs a spinning kick that knocks down everyone at once.

Dauragon is so quick that he may even block your attacks from the rear. When Dauragon is guarding, you can do one of two things: Use the Buster Throw (ES + h) to nullify his Guard, or perform the Combo Side Kick (h,h,h). There is a strong chance that Dauragon will drop his Guard while you are executing this move.

You should avoid moves that involve jumping, spinning, or sweeping the ground. Sion takes too long to recover his battle stance after performing such moves.

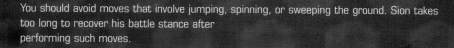

A Trinity Rush attack is useless against Dauragon, so launch combination attacks instead. Use the Torpedo Kick to launch Dauragon into the air. If you are swift enough, you can move Sion behind Dauragon's landing position. As soon as he starts to rise, launch him into the air again!

Although we've taken great pains and gone to some length to teach you a winning strategy, you must fight this battle swiftly and wisely. You should finish off Dauragon and still have 50% or more of your Life and Defense still intact. Otherwise, Sion probably won't last the second round!

Power Up!

Although the player is not allowed to save or switch bouncers between battles, a BP Exchange can occur. The player must wisely spend whatever Bouncer Points have been accumulated from the last fight.

If there are enough points for an Extra Skill, then go with Sion's Torpedo Kick or Floating Mine moves. Both moves prove to be extremely useful in countering Dauragon, especially while he is attempting to jab or thrust. While the Tornado Uppercut is extremely useful against Dauragon's constant Guard, the player will probably not amass enough BP to purchase it during the first game.

You may try to improve Sion's Power level. Spending BP on Defense or Life will lengthen the meter, but the player *will not recover* lost Life or Defense by upgrading either of these. By improving Power, you will be able to match Dauragon's increased speed and force in the next match.

BATTLE 27

Dauragon III (Boss)

BOSS

DAURAGON (OVERALLS) STATUS CHART

Status	Rank							
	G	F	E	D	C	B	A	S
Life	130	145	160	175	190	205	220	235
Power	100	114	128	142	157	171	185	200
Defense	100	112	125	138	151	164	177	190
BP	220	293	366	440	513	586	660	880

BOSS

DAURAGON (OVERALLS) EXTRA SKILLS

Name	Rank							
	G	F	E	D	C	B	A	S
Sonic Elbow	✳	✳	✳	✳	✳	✳	✳	✳
Dragon Spiral	✳	✳	✳	✳	✳	✳	✳	✳
Launcher	-	-	✳	✳	✳	✳	✳	✳
Jet Uppercut	-	-	-	-	✳	✳	✳	✳

The Desperate Hour

Dauragon is down, but not out. Whipping off his cumbersome overcoat, the despotic leader of the Mikado Corporation is now capable of more powerful moves, including the unblockable Jet Uppercut. You must not afford him the opportunity to use this.

Dauragon moves more quickly and attacks more frequently this time around. Spread out and surround Dauragon again, and use the Torpedo Kick often, if possible. The Floating Mine (ES + j), if available, also works well. When Dauragon is guarding, use the Buster Throw or launch a three-move combo attack to possibly lower his Guard.

Remember to constantly move, and keep Dauragon surrounded. However, it's much more difficult this time due to his unblockable Jet Uppercut. But if you keep moving, Dauragon will have a harder time performing this attack.

With Dauragon defeated, the game isn't quite over. The Ending Event Sequence will depend on which bouncer you chose for certain battles and certain scenarios in the game. There is a section in the Secrets section at the end of the Story Mode chapter that helps you understand how the endings play out.

VOLT

Age 27
Height 6'4"
Fighting Style Pro-Wrestling

VOLT KRUEGER

As a longtime bouncer at the bar, Volt acts as a big brother who, in a way, looks after his friends. Despite his intimidating appearance, he is gentle and peaceful in nature. A man of few words with a keen sense of duty, Volt spares nothing to fight for a friend or to protect someone to whom he is indebted.

In his younger days, Volt often brawled along with a gang of hooligans. He was regarded as a big brother by the young gang members. Once, he even involved himself in an assassination plot to protect his "brothers." After leaving the gang, he found a job at a private company.

Volt displays a curiously deep knowledge about the Mikado Corporation. Either he reads the *Daily COE* like a fanatic, or he has gained valuable inside information at a high price.

NO ESCAPE, CACTUAR!

The image on the back of Volt's jacket is a bit strange. The green character is a cactuar, a recurring enemy in Square's FINAL FANTASY series. Since it's crossed out and the words "No Escape!" are printed above the design, we can only suppose that Volt has little tolerance for cactuars!

VOLT'S MOVES LIST

Type	Name	Command	Base Damage
Jump	Hammer Drop	j	18
Jump	Flying Body Press	J	15
High	Right Hook	h	8
High	Double Hook	h,h	9
High	Triple Hook	h,h,h	12
High	Headbutt	H	23
High	Crushing Blow	h,H	24
High	Lightning Kneel Kick	Direction + h	18
Middle	Front Kick	m	9
Middle	Rolling Savate	M	15
Middle	Drop Kick	m,M	29
Middle	Running Lariat	Direction + m	21
Low	Foot Stomp	l	8
Low	Trip Kick	L	18
Low	Heavy Low Kick	l,L	20
ES1	Shoulder Uppercut	ES + h	30
ES2	Hammer Typhoon	ES + m	18
ES3	Lift Up Slam*	ES + l	21
ES4	Power Bridge*	ES + j	26
ES5	Cannonball Strike*	ES + h + m	28
ES6	Earthshaker*	ES + m + l	30
ES7	Giant Swing*	ES + l + j	33

*Throw Moves

VOLT'S STATUS UPGRADE BP COSTS

Status Raise	Life	Power	Defense
1-2	160	160	160
2-3	240	240	240
3-4	320	320	320
4-5	400	400	400
5-6	560	560	560
6-7	800	800	800
7-8	1200	1200	1200

VOLT'S EXTRA SKILLS BP COSTS

ES	Cost
Shoulder Uppercut	960
Hammer Typhoon	1000
Lift Up Slam	1200
Power Bridge	1500
Cannonball Strike	1800
Earthshaker	2400
Giant Swing	3500

VOLT'S STATUS LEVELS

Status	Lv1	Lv2	Lv3	Lv4	Lv5	Lv6	Lv7	Lv8
Life	105	122	139	156	173	190	207	225
Power	70	89	108	127	147	166	185	205
Defense	60	77	94	111	128	145	162	180

BATTLE STRATEGIES

BATTLE 1
"Fate" Bar

EVENT SEQUENCE

Things are slow at the bar.

Dominique brightens up Volt's day.

Mikado Special Forces invade FATE!

"They Weren't After *Me*?!"

This first battle strategy is written to teach you some basics about how Volt fights. Some strategies and tips discussed in this section can be applied to **all** of Volt's skirmishes. Other hints are more specific to this encounter.

Volt uses a weight-oriented, pro-wrestling style of fighting. Most of his moves will knock down an enemy, so Volt will spend a good deal of time waiting for opponents to get back up. His attacks are powerful, and he will KO enemies just as quickly as Sion or Kou, but with less work involved.

A quick study of Volt's list of combat moves shows that most of his more damaging combination moves are executed or begun with a light tap on an attack button. To have the full range of Volt's moves at your disposal, you must acquaint yourself with what exactly the difference is between a "light tap" and a "heavy tap."

LIGHT BUTTON TAP VS. HEAVY BUTTON TAP

A good way to determine the difference between a "light tap" and a "heavy tap" is the Sensitivity Configuration in the Options menu. Before starting a game, enter the Options menu and select "Controller Settings." Scroll down to the Sensitivity controls for your controller. Leave the sensitivity at Medium; it's the most flexible setting. Press the Square button, and the meter will measure the strength of your press. A "light tap" fills less than half the meter, and a "heavy tap" is any press that registers above half, no matter how quick.

The MSF (Mikado Special Forces) soldiers mean serious business, so you must mix some caution with skillfully executed attacks to win. The MSF are all quite a bit higher in Rank than your rookie Rank G character. However, Volt is the character that is **least likely** to get KO'd during this first battle since he starts out with the highest amount of Life. If Volt does get KO'd, though, this is the one time where the game will continue instead of ending.

Positioning Volt properly on the battlefield is extremely important in every fight. Never lose sight of your character in the fray. Move Volt to the forefront of the fighting area, and keep him visible. Always begin a battle by circling the enemy group until you find a lone opponent on the outskirts near the forefront, and fight your way inward.

Avoid pursuing enemies that flee or back into a crowd. Also, keep in mind that your attacks will propel an enemy backward, and you could get sucked into a crowd or even surrounded quite easily if you continue to knock them back. A good strategy is to always make the enemy that is **in front of you** the top priority, and do everything to stay out of the middle, where enemies can often attack you from behind.

The MSF can perform an evasive backflip that makes them difficult to attack. Use powerful moves and combos that propel Volt toward the enemy, such as the Running Lariat (Direction + m) or the Rolling Savate (M). Otherwise, run toward evasive enemies and raise your Guard. Wait for them to attack, and block it before you attempt to execute more attacks.

Enemies are positioned on the top and bottom levels. So after you KO the enemies in the loft, move Volt downstairs to engage the two MSF on the ground floor. Use Volt's Crushing Blow (h,H) or a Drop Kick (m,M) for big damage. If

two opponents attack at once, focus combination moves on one enemy until he goes down and press the R1 button to deflect any retaliatory blows. MSF are slow to raise their own defenses, so you are free to fire away after deflecting attacks.

"YOU'RE GOING DOWN!"

Since there are quite a few enemies in such confined quarters, make sure you use the Trinity Rush attack when available. Just listen for Kou to whistle, and press the R2 button to trigger the move. Although it looks like the trio teams up on one foe, actually **all** opponents are damaged in the attack.

Power Up!

Whether you remain conscious or not through your first battle, the first BP Exchange screen appears after the fight. Since the MSF rank fairly well against you, you should receive 41 or 50 points for each enemy you defeat.

After the battle, you will receive Bonus Points dependent upon your overall Game Rank. Since you start off at Rank G, you will receive 100 points for finishing the battle. Bonus Points received for battles increase as your Game Rank improves.

Exchanging BP for status improvement is generally more important than purchasing Extra Skills. Most of Volt's Extra Skills are throws, and only well-practiced expert players can execute such moves with finesse. Not only that, but Volt's Extra Skills are quite expensive compared to Kou's and Sion's.

Begin by increasing your Power level for 160 BP, so that your attacks and combos have more punch. Defense should be your next priority, since Volt has plenty of Life for the early stages of the game.

BATTLE 2
Central Square

EVENT SEQUENCE

Volt can't believe Dominique is the target.

Kou plays with his digital phone.

The trio heads for the MSD Cargo Train.

Interceptors appear outside the Station.

The MSF Are Back For More

In the first battle, Volt started in an optimum position on the outside of the fighting area and the enemies were surrounded. This time it's the other way around. You must first concentrate on positioning Volt where he can fight safely without getting surrounded. The MSF are much lower in Rank this time and much easier to fight, but staying in the middle of the ring is a bad idea.

Once Volt assumes fighting stance, move him around an attacking enemy and toward the gates, so that there is no danger of getting hit from behind. You can get to the outside more quickly by performing a Running Lariat (Direction + m); just make sure you turn around quickly since Volt will be facing the wrong way.

Focus on using Volt's more damaging combination moves, and use the Rolling Savate (M) and Triple Hook (h,h,h) attacks to stay close to evasive MSFs. If they backflip several times and get too far away, use the Running Lariat to catch up.

Getting double-teamed is a greater possibility in this fight. If you are, focus your attacks on one MSF at a time. Knock down one enemy, then move Volt to face the other enemy waiting nearby.

Most of the battle will probably occur in the lower courtyard area, but it's possible to lead enemies to the upper area. If you can't find any enemies and the fight is still ongoing, another bouncer has probably led an enemy upstairs.

BATTLE 3
Central Station

EVENT SEQUENCE

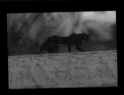
A mysterious black panther stalks the bouncers.

Guards outside the station spot the heroes!

Hey! What're you doing there!?

Volt doesn't need a ticket...

Oh, like you'll let us through if we tell you?

Turnstile Hoppers

Security Guards are the easiest to defeat in the Mikado chain of command. They are susceptible to the full range of Volt's combat moves, including the Headbutt (H) and Flying Body Press (J). However, using combination moves such as the Triple Hook (h,h,h) and the Drop Kick (m,M) will increase your chances of knocking out all three Guards yourself.

BATTLE 4
Central Station (Timed)

EVENT SEQUENCE

The MSD Cargo Train finishes loading.

The Security Guards are alerted.

Volt finds out there's a time limit.

Frenzied Fight

Kou mentions, there is a time limit to this battle. No timer is displayed on-screen, and the whistle doesn't sound until the events following battle. The fight will simply end after **45 seconds**. If you can KO all of the enemies on-screen before the time ends, then the heroes get oard the train with no problem. If not, then Sion misses the n and struggles to catch up.

characters all start the battle at the far left of the fighting e, and the Security Guards will meet your team near a lamp- t. Run Volt to the forefront of the cluster, and pick a guy near the edge. If you knock him down before their clus- spreads out, all the enemies will fall like dominoes! Also, you y get the opportunity to use a Trinity Rush attack during this ed struggle.

BATTLE 5
MSD Cargo Train

EVENT SEQUENCE

The bouncers stow away on the train.

Echidna unleashes her troops.

The bouncers leap into battle.

Protectors of the Cargo Train

Volt must fight for two rounds in this battle against two sets of three Security Guards. This is a good opportunity to pick up lots of BP and perhaps increase your Rank. Keep this in mind, because the first Boss fight is coming up!

Keep in mind that when a wall of enemies runs at a wall of bouncers, someone will get knocked down. In these close quarters, whoever gets knocked down will take down unwary characters with them, whether they be friend or foe.

To avoid getting flattened right away, deliver Volt's solid Rolling Savate (M) attack. This should knock down all the Guards right away. After doing so, surround the enemies with your bouncer friends. Now that the Guards are unprotected from the back, you may be able to knock them out more eas

BATTLE 6
Echidna (Boss) & Security Guards (2)

BOSS

ECHIDNA'S STATUS CHART

Status	Rank							
	G	F	E	D	C	B	A	S
Life	110	122	135	148	161	174	187	200
Power	80	93	107	120	134	147	161	175
Defense	90	106	122	139	155	172	188	205
BP	120	160	200	240	280	320	360	480

ECHIDNA'S EXTRA SKILLS

ES	Rank							
	G	F	E	D	C	B	A	S
Missile Kick	*	*	*	*	*	*	*	*
Cyclone Drive	-	*	*	*	*	*	*	*
Dead-End Carnival	-	-	*	*	*	*	*	*
Double Slap	-	-	-	*	*	*	*	*
Ambush Strike	-	-	-	-	*	*	*	*

RECOMMENDED CHOICE!

Choosing Volt for this fight is a rewarding decision. You'll hear a few more clues about Volt's past in the conversation that follows!

The Woman Warrior

After dusting off most of the train's security, the bouncers are confronted by the speeding train's female security administrator. Although the accompanying Security Guards are rather weak, don't underestimate Echidna's ability.

Make sure you guard from the outset of the fight. Then when it's clear, use Volt's Heavy Low Kick (I,L). You should rely on Volt's arsenal of Low and Middle attacks, because Echidna crouches down a lot. Successful attacks to counter Echidna's unique fighting style include the Rolling Savate (M) and the Flying Body Press (J).

Echidna is especially susceptible to Low attacks, but Volt's Low attacks are not terribly powerful. Performing the Trinity Rush attack on Echidna is quite helpful, so use it if given the chance.

...feating Echidna ends the battle immediately, even if the ...curity Guards are still standing. If you engage a Guard and ...ore Echidna, she may attack you from behind.

CARD KEY EVENT

After clearing the train of enemies, an attack by a mysterious fighter-plane disables the brakes. If the Card Key isn't found in time, the train will crash into the station, causing the rocket fuel tanks to detonate.

*If Volt is selected to find the Card Key, he only has 15 seconds to find it, so search quickly! There are three boxes in the train car: one to the left, one to the right, and one on the floor by the doorway. Simply move Volt to any box to have him search it. The Card Key is always inside the **last** box searched.*

If you find the Card Key in time, the rocket fuel tanks will disengage and the train will simply crash into the station. However, if the tanks are not released in time, the train will detonate upon impact and sea water will begin flooding the station. This changes the circumstances of the next long battle, causing the emergency shutters in the passageway to close. The enemies encountered are also tougher, as explained in the next section, Battle 7.

We don't have time for this!

I got it!

BATTLE 7
Emergency Passage (Normal Scenario)

EVENT SEQUENCE

The rocket fuel tanks are released.

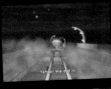

Yahoo! We did it!

The bouncers analyze their new situation.

We're in Mikado's domain now.

Volt leads the bouncers against security details.

Run for cover if you want to live.

A Minimum of Resistance

...etting through the emergency corridors is simple if you succeed in finding and using the Card Key onboard the MSD Cargo Train. There are ...r to five enemies on each floor, but only three will attack at the outset.

EMERGENCY PASSAGE (NORMAL)
CARD KEY FOUND IN TIME

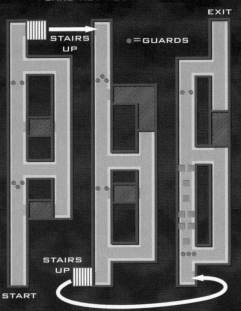

EXIT

STAIRS UP

= GUARDS

STAIRS UP

START

The reinforcements will arrive shortly, so it's important to take out the first wave before your trio gets outnumbered.

Some of the guards are wearing black vests and listening to headsets. The Security Chiefs (the ones with the black vests) are much tougher than the other foes. They are quicker to counterattack and more likely to block your moves. Since you have three floors of enemies to fight with only one full Life bar, you must be very cautious.

If you are unable to neutralize the first wave of attackers before the backup arrives, then remember to use a Trinity Rush attack if you hear a signal from your fellow bouncer.

After disposing of all the enemies (check the enemy status bar in the upper-right corner), run to the end of the corridor and up the stairs the next level. If you can't find your way, run toward a wall, look for a white arrow, and follow the direction it's pointing (or refer to the map

Don't wait for comrades who lag behind; they will be upstairs already when the next round of battle starts. Reaching the large door marked "EXIT" will end this battle.

RECOMMENDED PATH!

Finding the Card Key and disconnecting the rocket fuel cars from the train in time makes the battles in the Emergency Passage much easier. If you don't fin the Card Key in time, then you must contend with more difficult enemies in greater numbers, plus you have to outrun closing emergency shutters and follow twisting corridors.

BATTLE 7

Emergency Passage
(Closing Shutters Scenario)

EVENT SEQUENCE

olt can't find the ard Key in time.

We're jumping off as soon as we reach the station!

The train destroys the station.

Sea water floods the corridors.

The emergency shutters are closing!

o, Volt Couldn't Find the Card Key...

ou don't find the Card Key, the scenario inside the MSD Station is ered as sea water floods the area. The emergency shutters slam shut nind you, and several corridor sections are already sealed off.

e first battle is fairly simple, but take greater precautions when fighting e Security Chief. After the fight, Volt must run under a series of closing utter doors before they shut. This is easily accomplished by using the alog Stick instead of the Directional Button. Continue running forward d around the corner until you catch up to your buddies.

EMERGENCY PASSAGE (ALTERNATE)
CARD KEY NOT FOUND IN TIME

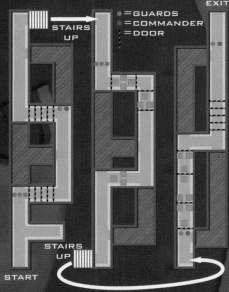

EXIT

STAIRS UP

=GUARDS
=COMMANDER
=DOOR

STAIRS UP

START

the next round, two more enemies come charging in from the distance. e of them is a Commander, an enemy that you will only encounter in this ernate scenario. Commanders can be hard to take down, largely due to eir advanced Defense and Power stats.

best to fight Commanders h your entire team. Take any minor enemies (like e lowly Security Guards), d then surround the mmander. While guarding, k for an opportunity to hit backside.

other corridor with closing shutters must be outrun. Turn Volt to right and continue down the corridor to the steps. Then go up flights of steps and down a short stretch of hallway to reach ur buddies. You must defeat all of the enemies on this floor to d this battle.

BATTLE 8
Air-Carrier

EVENT SEQUENCE

Volt opens the Emergency Exit doors.

Air-Carriers are searching the area.

The bouncers hitch a ride.

"We're Taking This Air-Carrier!"

Commandeering a Mikado Air-Carrier may prove to be a foolhardy idea. Carrier Soldiers are tough commandos in the organization's ranks. Your group is half-surrounded at the beginning of the match. Raising your Guard at the start of the fight is imperative.

Luckily, Volt is already at the forefront at the start of this battle. Take on the soldier in the bottom-right corner first. Hit him with attacks like the Headbutt (H) or Rolling Savate (M).

With Carrier Soldiers, the best strategy is to keep your Guard up and let them perform one or two moves before hitting back. Carrier Soldiers attack more often and more viciously than previous enemies. But in these close quarters, if you hit an enemy with a move such as the Rolling Savate (M), then you just might send him flying into his buddies.

Due to the scrolling backgrounds, using the Trinity Rush attack on the Air-Carrier is a visual feast, as well as a neck-twisting damage-fest.

BATTLE 9
Hanging Garden

EVENT SEQUENCE

The Air-Carrier flies up the Mikado Building.

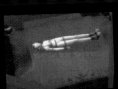

Sion locates Dominique.

Volt crash-lands the carrier.

Watchdogs are alerted to the heroes' presence.

Rocky Landing

Upon crash-landing the Air-Carrier, the trio is spotted by the Watchdogs known as "Bakilla." MSF soldiers are also dispatched to help the cyborg pups.

the start of the fight, knock down the closest Watchdog with a Trip Kick (L) followed by several Foot Stomps (I) and Heavy Low Kick combos]. If one gets behind you while you're fighting an MSF, it will knock you into the dirt.

can fight Mikado's secret soldiers with the same tactics used in previous encounters. Use the Crushing Blow (h,H) or Rolling Savate (M) en they're standing in front of you. If they perform a backflip, use Volt's Running Lariat (Direction + m) or the Flying Body Press (J). Even if blow doesn't connect, the move places Volt in better fighting position.

BATTLE 10

Mugetsu (Boss) & MSF Soldiers (4)

MUGETSU W/MASK STATUS CHART

Status	Rank							
	G	F	E	D	C	B	A	S
Life	110	124	138	152	167	181	195	210
Power	90	105	121	137	152	168	184	200
Defense	70	84	98	112	127	141	155	170
BP	150	200	250	300	350	400	450	600

MUGETSU W/MASK EXTRA SKILLS

ES	Rank							
	G	F	E	D	C	B	A	S
Ren-Getsu	-	-	*	*	*	*	*	*
Gen-Getsu (Hell)	*	*	*	*	*	*	*	*
Gen-Getsu (Heaven)	*	*	*	*	*	*	*	*
Hi-Getsu	-	-	-	-	*	*	*	*

The Psycho Man

Just as Volt predicts, Mugetsu arrives at the scene with his sanity decaying at a rapid pace. The MSF leader fights like a wild animal, taking on the nearest bouncer with reckless abandon. Volt can't become the center of Mugetsu's focus, or he'll get knocked all over the combat area.

You will never get the girl back!

Fight the multiple MSF soldiers with the tactics you've used up to this point. Your best moves are the Crushing Blow (h,H) and Rolling Savate (M). If they use a backflip, perform the Running Lariat (Direction + m) or the Flying Body Press (J).

Through the early part of the battle, focus on Mugetsu only [when] he happens to draw near. Then give him a few punches or a Headbutt (H), something really strong to knock him away. T[hen] turn back and continue fighting the lesser foes. Don't leave [an] active MSF on your flank, or the foe and Mugetsu will knock you back and forth.

During the fight, listen for the audio signal from your teammate so you can perform a Trinity Rush attack. As the enemy forces dwindle, it will be easier to focus on the madman.

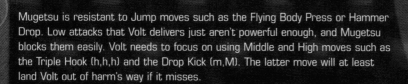

Mugetsu is resistant to Jump moves such as the Flying Body Press or Hammer Drop. Low attacks that Volt delivers just aren't powerful enough, and Mugetsu blocks them easily. Volt needs to focus on using Middle and High moves such as the Triple Hook (h,h,h) and the Drop Kick (m,M). The latter move will at least land Volt out of harm's way if it misses.

BATTLE 11
Dauragon (Boss) & Black Panther

EVENT SEQUENCE

Sion finds a way inside the dome.

Dauragon says goodbye to Wong.

The villain offers to fight one-handed.

BOSS BOSS BOSS BOSS

ONE-ARMED DAURAGON'S STATUS CHART

Status	Rank							
	G	F	E	D	C	B	A	S
Life	120	134	148	162	177	191	205	220
Power	70	88	107	125	144	162	181	200
Defense	70	82	95	108	121	134	147	160
BP	110	146	183	220	256	293	330	440

ONE-ARMED DAURAGON'S EXTRA SKILLS

ES	Rank							
	G	F	E	D	C	B	A	S
Whirlwind Kick	*	*	*	*	*	*	*	*
Crescent Moon Slash	*	*	*	*	*	*	*	*
Triple Rave Kick	-	-	-	-	*	*	*	*
Elbow Spear	-	-	*	*	*	*	*	*

??? (BLACK PANTHER) STATUS CHART

Status	Rank							
	G	F	E	D	C	B	A	S
Life	100	113	127	140	154	167	181	195
Power	70	84	98	112	127	141	155	170
Defense	90	105	121	137	152	168	184	200
BP	120	160	200	240	280	320	360	480

Master Mikado's Folly

The head of the Mikado Corporation is anything but humble. Binding his right arm behind him in chains, he claims that he can still defeat all three bouncers... which may well be the case!

Dauragon performs a powerful spin kick that will knock down everyone, and follows it with a Reverse Sweep and a Double Talon Kick. Watch out for the Black Panther circling the area, trying to attack the bouncers from behind.

Focus your attention on Dauragon. Position Volt behind the flamboyant executive and try to surround him with the bouncers at all times. Stand with your Guard up until Dauragon turns his back to you. When this occurs, hit him with a Triple Hook (h,h,h) or the Crushing Blow (h,H).

Avoid using any running attacks (the Running Lariat, the Drop Kick, and the Lightning Kneel Kick almost always miss), and stay away from moves involving wide swings or spins. The Flying Body Press can be effective, but doesn't cause much damage. Avoid attempting combo moves from the front; Dauragon readily shows that he is capable of countering them.

If Dauragon seems intent on beating your Guard down, then back aw[ay] as best you can. Upon doing so, he will most likely turn his attention back to the other bouncers. This provides a good chance to hit him with a Rolling Savate (M).

Take note that the Black Panther is worth more BP than Dauragon! The only problem is that fighting this creature is second in priority. You can only attack it with Low blows, the best move being the Heavy Low Kick combo (l,L). If you plan to attack the panther first, knock it away from Dauragon and fight it one-on-one. The best strategy for your first time through the game is to focus your attacks on Dauragon, and only turn your attention to the Black Panther if it gets directly behind Volt. The battle ends when Dauragon is defeated, regardless if the panther is still conscious.

BATTLE 16

Mikado Building—Enhancement Surgery Area

EVENT SEQUENCE

Volt finds himself strapped to surgical equipment.

Breaking free, he lets himself out.

Two MSF soldiers bar Volt's escape.

The Butchers' Domain

When Volt is selected after the Dauragon/Black Panther fight, a scenario begins where he must fight Battle 16 and the two-round Battle 17 alone. Althoug[h] there are breaks between battles to exchange BP, save your game and restore Life and Defense, there is no opportunity to choose a different character.

Whereas Sion's Mikado Building adventure involves navigation and Kou's is steeped in espionage and stealth, Volt's experience is more suited t[o] his taste. The big bouncer's only objective is to pound, slam, and stuff everyone that gets in his way!

The first battle is simple enough. Volt is double-teamed, but if you use the catwalks to your advantage you can keep your attackers at bay. Use the Rolling Savate (M) to knock down both enemies. Then move Volt to the left section of the walk, and stay out of the wide intersection. The MSF can only confront Volt from one direction! They must also stand close together, which makes knocking them down much simpler.

Use moves such as Volt's Triple Hook (h,h,h) and Crushing Blow (h,H). After disposing of the duo, move Volt down the long stairway to the left and through the door.

BATTLE 17

Mikado Building— Bio-Plant/Robot Factory

The Fearsome Arena

After the last battle, it's no surprise that you are suddenly faced with overwhelming adversity. No matter how good you are, Volt is bound to take a few kicks in this match.

The only tactical advantage you can maintain in this open area is to keep Volt's back against a wall. This makes it more difficult for the MSF and 'bots to surround him. However, since most of Volt's moves propel him forward, it's easier said than done.

Most importantly, take out the P-101 robots first. They can charge at Volt from a great distance and easily knock him down. When one gets in front of Volt, continuously perform the Rolling Savate (M). With the robots out of action, Volt can use moves like the Drop Kick (m,M) and the Flying Body Press (J) to knock down and damage multiple opponents at once.

Tactical Nightmare

The next battle features a myriad of MSF appearing in one location. How can Volt possibly take on this abundance of enemies and come out without a scratch? By using the tactics described below, that's how!

As the fight begins, *stay right where you are— do not move into the larger area.* This prevents the MSF from surrounding you. The MSF and Elites on the lower level will charge at Volt. However, if Volt remains in the narrower section, they won't be able to spread out. Use a Rolling Savate (M) on the closest one. This should cause them to all fall down and take damage!

Avoid venturing into the large area; instead, move into the narrow walkway and wait for the MSF to cluster in front of Volt again. Continue to knock them down until only one or two remain. Then pick off the stragglers with combo moves like the Crushing Blow (J,H) and the Drop Kick (m,M).

After disposing of the larger group, move Volt to the back of the platform and up the stairs to the higher level. It's possible to engage one of the remaining enemies without the other getting involved. Simply run along the right side of the platform to where the MSF Elite should be standing. You should be able to take out this guy before the lower MSF gets involved. Just don't allow Volt to travel too close to the second enemy when fighting the Elite.

Mugetsu (Boss), MSF Soldiers (2), & MSF Elite (2)

EVENT SEQUENCE

Volt finds a disturbing report.

Sion is having some difficulties.

Volt finds a cannonball to launch.

Mugetsu is humiliated!

BOSS

MUGETSU W/MASK STATUS CHART

	Rank							
Status	G	F	E	D	C	B	A	S
Life	110	124	138	152	167	181	195	210
Power	90	105	121	137	152	168	184	200
Defense	70	84	98	112	127	141	155	170
BP	150	200	250	300	350	400	450	600

MUGETSU W/MASK EXTRA SKILLS

	Rank							
ES	G	F	E	D	C	B	A	S
Ren-Getsu	-	-	*	*	*	*	*	*
Gen-Getsu (Hell)	*	*	*	*	*	*	*	*
Gen-Getsu (Heaven)	*	*	*	*	*	*	*	*
Hi-Getsu	-	-	-	-	*	*	*	*

Everyone's Gotten Sloppy

Following the battle in the Robot Factory, move Volt through a short hallway section into the Data Room on 66F. After perusing some scattered files, Volt takes the stairs up to the Executive Level. Run down the red carpet until Volt spots Sion suffering at the hands of Mugetsu. After his boisterous entrance, Volt is ready to teach the psycho-borg another lesson.

This guy's lost his mind...!

Like the previous encounter at the Hanging Garden, the best approach is to adopt Mugetsu's roaming-fighting method. Initially, concentrate mo of your efforts against the MSF and Elite soldiers, using the same tactics as before. Use the Triple Hook (h,h,h) and the Rolling Savate (M) wh fighting in close range. If they perform a backflip, use the Running Lariat (Direction + m) to catch up to them. Try the Flying Body Press (J) on multiple enemies if Volt gets double-teamed.

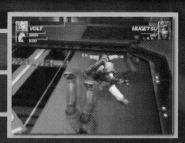

Avoid fighting Mugetsu unless he happens to draw near, and focus on the first enemy that engages Volt, no matter who it is. Keep after that enemy until he gets KO'd. Position Volt so that his back is near a wall; avoid going in the center. Another good place to fight is between the couch and the desk, but only after several MSF have been KO'd. Use a Trinity Rush attack whenever possible.

helpful to get all the MSF and Elite enemies out of the way so that you can tame Mugetsu. Avoid using the Headbutt, the Hammer Drop, or Lightning Heel Kick because they are too slow to work on Mugetsu.

Running Lariat (Direction + m) often goes straight over Mugetsu, so use it sparingly (if at all). Focus on using the same attacks used on the SF against Mugetsu. Low attacks just aren't powerful enough, and Mugetsu blocks them easily. When Mugetsu is defeated, the battle ends ardless of the other enemies' status.

BATTLE 20
Rocket Tower 6F to 2F

EVENT SEQUENCE

Dominique is revived.

The Rocket Tower goes on full alert.

The team decides to split up.

Dominique knows Volt will protect her.

Jammin' Paradise

hile Dominique is fine with Volt accompanying her, she still seems disappointed. The big bodyguard has an incredibly long and difficult fight ead. The bouncer chosen to accompany the young lady through the Rocket Tower must survive a multi-level gauntlet of robotic sentinels that ve been switched from work mode to attack mode. Keep in mind the following conditions:

You must survive all levels with only *one* Life bar; no breaks or refills.

Dominique must survive as well. If she gets KO'd before you reach the final exit, it's "Game Over."

If Volt's or Dominique's Life meters get down to 25% or less, you'd best stop fighting the rest of the robots and make a break for the final exit.

Against all robots, you should choose single, non-combo moves that you can repeat quickly. Avoid using moves where Volt rears back or jumps high in the air. These take too much time to execute and have a long recovery time. The robots *will retaliate* in between your attacks if given the chance.

aracters with higher Ranks will be better suited to take on every robot and enemy in the Rocket Tower. Since Volt's Life meter starts off high- than the other two bouncers, he is ideally suited for combat here. But still, even if you've been spending BP and have reached F or E Rank timated), you'll need to pick your battles wisely and skip a few enemies entirely. This section will give you pointers on who to fight, who not to t, and how to survive.

On the first platform, you fight a trio of robots. With an LD-15 (the big orange robot) in front and one moving in from behind, you must prevent Volt and Dominique from getting pounded right at the start. Run over to the side wall and lead Dominique around the platform to the e stairs. If you decide to attack them, eliminate the little P-101 robot first and keep Volt out of danger.

On the next level down, you find a gray, humanoid robot called an MC-07. Use the Triple Hook (h,h,h) to push it back, followed by a Crushing Blow (h,H) to finish the job. Since most of this robot's moves are performed up high with its arms, Volt can interrupt its attacks in mid-motion by performing a simple Trip Kick (L).

While fighting the MC-07, the LD-15 is moving in from the rear. Don't get surrounded or you'll take some serious damage. If the MC-07 is knocked behind the LD-15 by your blows, then Volt should face-off against the larger worker droid instead.

Fighting LD-15s is tricky. They have very long Life meters, so attack them with short, non-combo moves such as the Rolling Savate (M) or the Crushing Blow (h,H).

Proceed up the stairs to take on another MC-07, and then descend the next set of stairs and **run past** the next LD-15 to the exit. Only whe you are replaying the game with a higher Rank should you tangle with it.

At the bottom of the stairs on the 4th floor is a simple Security Guard. To defeat him, just make sure you wait for him to get back up each tim you knock him down. Advanced players may want to proceed up the stairs to take on two MC-07s. Naturally, low-level bouncers should avoid t risky fight.

Down the stairs, a Security Chief engages Volt. Keep your Guard up until he attacks, and then retaliate with a powerful move like the Drop Kic (m,M) or the Crushing Blow (h,H). If you knock him down the stairs, pursue him and be ready when he gets back up.

Take the stairs down to Level 3. Move to the left and locate the two bridge structures connected to the next platform. **Avoid** fighting with the LD-15 blocking the right bridge, and instead lead Dominique toward the MC-07. You can fight this lone robot, but be warned that another MC-07 and an LD-15 are in the area.

re's another set of bridges that takes you to the next platform. You can avoid confrontation with LD-15 and the MC-07 altogether by crossing on the left-hand bridge. To the left of their posi- is the stairwell down to the final level.

Move Volt straight ahead from the bottom of the steps to encounter a lone MC-07 that is easy to take out. Beyond it is the green-colored lift that marks the exit.

Advanced bouncers with higher Ranks may want to take out the MC-07 and the LD-15 at the opposite end of this platform before leaving, just to acquire the extra BP!

BATTLE 21

PD-4 (Boss)

BOSS **BOSS**

PD-4'S STATUS CHART

Status	Rank							
	G	F	E	D	C	B	A	S
Life	120	134	148	162	177	191	205	220
Power	90	102	115	128	141	154	167	180
Defense	95	107	120	133	146	159	172	185
BP	170	226	283	340	396	453	510	680

PD-4'S EXTRA SKILLS

Skill Name	G	F	E	D	C	B	A	S
Thunder Fall	-	-	*	*	*	*	*	*
Lightning Whip	*	*	*	*	*	*	*	*
Elbow Spin Break	*	*	*	*	*	*	*	*
Lightning Viper	-	-	-	-	*	*	*	*

Superweapon My Foot!

Volt and Dominique run into PD-4 on the lowest level of the Rocket Tower. This evil prototype bionoid craves only death and destruction. While it has been ordered to retrieve Dominique, Sion and Kou arrive to help Volt prevent that from happening.

-4 charges at Volt immediately, so raise your Guard and ect the initial attack. PD-4 uses long, multi-hit combo ves but needs time to recover after attacking. Keep your rd up the whole time it attacks, and attack only when PD-4 ses to recover. Volt's best moves to use against PD-4 are Triple Hook (h,h,h), the Crushing Blow (h,H), and the ing Savate (M). The Drop Kick (m,M) is also effective, but y from the rear.

Try to coax the bionoid into a circle between Volt, Sion, an Kou. It's best to keep PD-4 surrounded, so that it doesn't know which side to defend against. Each chance you get, u Volt's most powerful moves and combos.

Naturally, we're going to suggest that you use a Trinity Rush attack. There should be several opportunities, since you'll probably spend most of the fight standing with your Guard up.

BATTLE 22
Rocket Tower—Basement

EVENT SEQUENCE

Mugetsu nabs Dominique— again!

Volt shares a little info with Sion.

It's the debut of the LD-X1.

More Robot Playthings

The black loader robot is slightly stronger and has a higher Life meter than the other robots. Take out the LD-15s first using Volt's quick attacks with short recovery times, such as the Crushing Blow (h,H) or the Rolling Savate (M). Any other moves may push the loaders too far away.

Attack the LD-X1 with your whole group, and position Volt behind it. When the robot rears back to attack, be ready t block.

Power Up!

If you've been exchanging your BP for mostly status upgrades throughout the game, then your Bouncers should be in good shape for the las four battles—which are all Boss fights!

When your BP and Bonus Points are tallied up this time, treat yourself to one of Volt's Extra Skills if you have enough. Learn either the Shoulder Uppercut or the Hammer Typhoon. Either of the aforementioned moves will help out immensely in the uphill struggle that follows.

BATTLE 23

Echidna (Boss) & LD-X1 Robots (2)

ECHIDNA'S STATUS CHART

Status	Rank							
	G	F	E	D	C	B	A	S
Life	110	122	135	148	161	174	187	200
Power	80	93	107	120	134	147	161	175
Defense	90	106	122	139	155	172	188	205
BP	120	160	200	240	280	320	360	480

ECHIDNA'S EXTRA SKILLS

ES	Rank							
	G	F	E	D	C	B	A	S
Missile Kick	✳	✳	✳	✳	✳	✳	✳	✳
Cyclone Drive	-	✳	✳	✳	✳	✳	✳	✳
Dead-End Carnival	-	-	✳	✳	✳	✳	✳	✳
Double Slap	-	-	-	✳	✳	✳	✳	✳
Ambush Strike	-				✳	✳	✳	✳

RECOMMENDED CHOICE!

While matching Volt's slow and thunderous fighting style to Echidna's flying feet of fury is a bit difficult, using Volt to fight this battle causes the scene afterward to be a bit longer and more informative. Echidna also makes surprise appearances in later cut-scenes!

Woman's Wrath

e red-headed vixen is back! This time, she's serious about killing Volt and has brought along better pport. The two LD-X1s are like giant moving walls, and they've been programmed to assist Echidna in nihilating everyone!

I've had enough of your mockery! You haven't changed at all.

Raise your Guard immediately to avoid Echidna's Capoeira spinning fighter moves. They're guaranteed to knock down an unguarded fighter! As she rises from her attack, hit her with Volt's Trip Kick (L).

While she's down, you may need to engage the nearest LD-X1. Use the Rolling Savate (M) multiple times to push the loader outward, breaking up the cluster. If Echidna sneaks up behind Volt, move around the loader so that it's between you and her.

not a bad idea to take out both machines first, plus it helps increase r BP score as well. However, if Echidna comes after Volt, lead her or ck her away from the robots. Staying alive is more important than BP, d Echidna makes it difficult to concentrate on anything but her when e's around.

ce Echidna hovers so close to the ground, rely on moves like the Rolling Savate (M) and the Heavy Low Kick (I,L). That's why we suggested that t learn the Hammer Typhoon or Shoulder Uppercut after the last battle. It provides another option to use against her. Otherwise, keep using a nity Rush attack every time you hear the signal. When Echidna dives for the floor, press the R1 button to block her flurry of attacks!

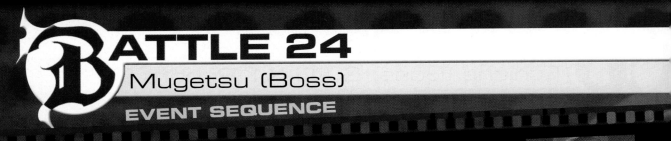

BATTLE 24
Mugetsu (Boss)
EVENT SEQUENCE

The Galeos launches.

The bouncers grab a ride.

Mugetsu leaps aboard the Air-Carrier!

BOSS

MUGETSU W/O MASK STATUS CHART

Status	Rank							
	G	F	E	D	C	B	A	S
Life	120	134	148	162	177	191	205	220
Power	100	115	131	147	162	178	194	210
Defense	65	79	93	107	122	136	150	165
BP	180	240	300	360	420	480	540	720

BOSS

MUGETSU W/O MASK EXTRA SKILLS

ES	Rank							
	G	F	E	D	C	B	A	S
Shi-Getsu	-	✳	✳	✳	✳	✳	✳	✳
Fuku-Getsu	-	-	-	-	✳	✳	✳	✳
Ka-Getsu	-	-	✳	✳	✳	✳	✳	✳
Ren-Getsu	✳	✳	✳	✳	✳	✳	✳	✳

Psycho Boy Returns!

Commandeering an Air-Carrier and sneaking onboard the space shuttle Galeos should be a snap for Volt and the bouncers. But the psychopathic Mugetsu turns up for one more battle. This time he's gone completely mental, and flings himself onto the transport. Without the constraints of caution and reason, you'll find that Mugetsu is a much more lethal opponent than in previous engagements.

First, "Who's going to fly the Air-Carrier?" Since this strategy is for Volt to fight, let one of the other two handle it.

As the fight begins, raise your Guard and wait for Mugetsu to attack. He will most likely perform a Crazy Drill, where he instantly becomes horizontal and fires himself like a torpedo. It takes a moment for Mugetsu to recover from this move, so flatten him using a Flying Body Press (J).

Me!? Fine, fine, I'll do it!

As Mugetsu gets back up, position him between Volt and your fellow bouncer. If he goes after your partner, kick him from the rear. If not, raise your Guard and wait for him to attack again, and then perform another direct, non-combo move such as the Rolling Savate (M) or the Trip Kick (L). Volt's combo moves are too slow to use against Mugetsu in his hyper state. The only one that has a chance is the Triple Hook (h,h,h).

ce there are only two bouncers in this fight, you cannot use a Trinity Rush attack. Also, you don't
t to let your partner get KO'd. Taking on Mugetsu in his psychotic state is a little more than you
 handle alone.

vare also of the Ren-Getsu, a move where Mugetsu begins spinning like a top above the ground. If
 does this in front of Volt, keep your Guard up the whole time to avoid any damage.

Mugetsu rarely blocks, but attacks swiftly and often. If
Volt has the Shoulder Uppercut Extra Skill, use it to
counter Mugetsu's constant barrage of two-handed
chops. Volt crouches right under the raving lunatic and
propels him high into the air.

BATTLE 25
Black Panther (Sub-Boss)

BLACK PANTHER'S STATUS CHART

Status	Rank							
	G	F	E	D	C	B	A	S
Life	100	113	127	140	154	167	181	195
Power	70	84	98	112	127	141	155	170
Defense	90	105	121	137	152	168	184	200
BP	120	160	200	240	280	320	360	480

BLACK PANTHER'S EXTRA SKILLS

Name	Rank							
	G	F	E	D	C	B	A	S
Griffin Talons	-	-	*	*	*	*	*	*
Meteor Storm	*	*	*	*	*	*	*	*
Griffin Tail	-	-	-	-	*	*	*	*
Spinning Rush	*	*	*	*	*	*	*	*
Wild Fang	-	-	*	*	*	*	*	*
Shape Shift	*	*	*	*	*	*	*	*

ady of Shadows

board the Galeos, the mysterious Black Panther leaps into the path and prevents the bouncers from
ching the control room. Looks like Dauragon's strange pet has an overwhelming need to protect
.

This is no ordinary panther!

Since the panther is so low to the ground, only Low attacks
prove to be effective. Repeatedly attack the beast with Foot
Stomps (I) and the Heavy Low Kick combo (I,L). When the
Black Panther growls, press the R1 button to block its upcoming attacks.

Several times during the battle, the panther shape-shifts into a female human form. This bizarre woman attacks with sweeping tai-chi based attacks, so guard until the attacks subside. Knock her to the ground with the Crushing Blow (h,H), or launch her high into the air with the Shoulder Uppercut (ES + h) (if you have it).

BATTLE 26
Dauragon II (Boss)

DAURAGON'S STATUS CHART

Status	Rank							
	G	F	E	D	C	B	A	S
Life	125	140	155	170	185	200	215	230
Power	80	97	114	131	148	165	182	200
Defense	80	94	108	122	137	151	165	180
BP	150	200	250	300	350	400	450	600

DAURAGON'S EXTRA SKILLS

Name	Rank							
	G	F	E	D	C	B	A	S
Whirlwind Kick	*	*	*	*	*	*	*	*
Crescent Moon Slash	*	*	*	*	*	*	*	*
Dragon Claw	-	-	*	*	*	*	*	*
Dragon Blitz	*	*	*	*	*	*	*	*
Wyvern's Sting	-	-	-	-	*	*	*	*

King of Fighters

So, do you think you're brawny enough to take Dauragon on when he uses *both* hands? Sure you are!

I will avenge Master Mikado...

The bouncer you choose for this battle must fight *two* rounds with the well-trained martial arts master. There is no opportunity between fights to select a different bouncer, and your Life bar will not refill between battles. Also, this battle can severely drain your bouncer's Defense meter. Without the ability to block, Dauragon will make quick work of you, and Volt will have a hard time making it through the second round.

The control room of the Galeos provides ample floor space for sparring, but there are curved areas to the left and right of Dominique's position that you need to watch out for.

At the start of the fight, it's best to surround Dauragon with your bouncers. Keep up your Guard until he turns his back, and then execute a fierce combo attack such as the Crushing Blow (h,H) or Triple Hook (h,h,h).

Move around frequently and then settle back into Guard stance to protect Volt. You want to keep Dauragon surrounded constantly by the bouncers. Sion and Kou will usually take up positions in a triangular shape, as long as Volt keeps positioning himself behind Dauragon.

With bouncers on all sides, Dauragon will attack and defend in every direction. He can even perform a spinning kick that knocks down everyone at once.

Dauragon is so quick that he might block your attacks from the rear. When Dauragon is guarding, you can do one of two things: Use one of Volt's throws to nullify his Guard, or perform a three-move combo like the Triple Hook (h,h,h). Dauragon may drop his Guard while defending against the Triple Hook, thus enabling you to catch him with the last and most powerful punch.

Avoid moves that involve jumping, rearing back or crouching low to the ground. Volt takes too long to execute these moves and his recovery time is even longer.

The Trinity Rush attack is useless against Dauragon. He breaks free of it each time. When Dauragon gets knocked down, quickly run Volt to the other side so that your bouncers are surrounding him again. If Dauragon seems to be attacking Volt over and over, try to back away in between volleys. He will eventually turn his attention back to the other bouncers, giving you a great opportunity to strike.

Use the Shoulder Uppercut if possible. When done properly, you should be able to move Volt behind Dauragon's landing position. As soon as he starts to rise, launch him into the air again!

Although we've taken great pains and gone to some length to provide some winning strategy, you must fight this battle swiftly and wisely. You should finish the first round with 50% or more of your Life and Defense still intact. Otherwise, Volt will have a hard time surviving the second round.

Power Up!

Although you can't save or switch bouncers between battles, a BP Exchange occurs. The player must wisely spend whatever Bouncer Points have been accumulated from the last fight.

If there are enough points for an Extra Skill, then choose Volt's Shoulder Uppercut or Hammer Typhoon moves, if you haven't already purchased them. The first move is extremely useful at countering Dauragon, especially while he's attempting to jab or thrust. You can use the Hammer Typhoon on Dauragon while he's blocking, as the second hit will most likely catch him off-guard.

If you don't have enough BP for an Extra Skill, then improve Volt's Power level. Spending BP on Defense or Life will lengthen the meter, but the player *will not recover* lost Life or Defense by upgrading either of these.

BATTLE 27
Dauragon III (Boss)

DAURAGON (OVERALLS) STATUS CHART

Status	Rank							
	G	F	E	D	C	B	A	S
Life	130	145	160	175	190	205	220	235
Power	100	114	128	142	157	171	185	200
Defense	100	112	125	138	151	164	177	190
BP	220	293	366	440	513	586	660	880

DAURAGON (OVERALLS) EXTRA SKILLS

Name	Rank							
	G	F	E	D	C	B	A	S
Sonic Elbow	*	*	*	*	*	*	*	*
Dragon Spiral	*	*	*	*	*	*	*	*
Launcher	-	-	*	*	*	*	*	*
Jet Uppercut	-	-	-	-	*	*	*	*

The Desperate Hour

After the initial onslaught, Dauragon rips off his cumbersome overcoat ready to fight again. This time he possesses the unblockable Jet Uppercut; you must not allow him the opportunity to use it.

Don't be so arrogant, Dauragon...!

Dauragon moves more quickly and attacks more frequently in round two. As was the case earlier, surround Dauragon with all three bouncers and use the Shoulder Uppercut (if possible). The Hammer Typhoon also works well against Dauragon's Guard, because the second blow might connect even if the first is thwarted.

It's important to stay on the move, while establishing a perimeter around Dauragon. This proves much more difficult this time, since he will launch your comrades in every direction with his unblockable Jet Uppercut. If Dauragon performs the Launcher move or the Dragon Spiral on another bouncer, hit him from the rear while he's vulnerable to cause some serious damage.

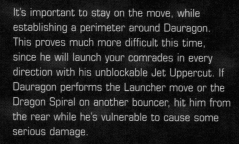

Upon defeating Dauragon, the game isn't quite over yet. The Ending Event Sequence depends upon which bouncer you chose for certain battles and certain scenarios in the game. There is a portion of the "Secrets" section at the end of this chapter that helps you understand how the endings play out. Also, stay tuned for Volt's surprising and unique Epilogue, which rounds out the story nicely.

KOU

Age 25
Height 6'0"
Fighting Style Tae Kwon Do

KOU LEIFOH

Born into wealth, Kou chose to abandon the shackles of prosperity in favor of a life of training and discipline. Studying martial arts from a very young age, Kou is a master of Tae Kwon Do. Why a person of his education and background would desire to get a full-body tattoo and become bouncer in a rough-and-tumble Dog Street bar is something of a mystery. But that's Kou, a man of painfully obvious contradictions.

Although physically weaker than his fellow bouncers at FATE, Kou is far more advanced in technique and can utilize a greater number of moves.

Kou's attire is always flashy and chic, as is permanently exhibited in the full-body tattoo that extends from his ankles all the way up to his forehead. In accordance with his looks, he's a bit of a smooth-talker and a wisecracker.

KOU'S MOVES LIST

Type	Name	Command	Base Damage
Jump	Rolling Stomp	j	18
Jump	Spin Kick	J	16
Jump	Tiger Side Kick	Direction + j	9
Jump	Double Side Kick	Direction + j (x2)	20
High	Right Jab	h	8
High	Left Jab	h,h	9
High	Triple Jab	h,h,h	16
High	High Roundhouse Kick	H	12
High	Double Roundhouse Kick	H,h	12
High	Triple Roundhouse Kick	H,h,h	19
High	Uppercut	h,H	21
Middle	Forward Kick	m	11
Middle	Spinning Heel Drop	M	16
Middle	Heel Snap	m,M	26
Low	Low Reverse Kick	l	8
Low	Spinning Trip Kick	L	14
Low	Reverse Trip Kick	l,L	19
Low	Slider	Direction + l	12
ES1	Heel Smash	ES + l	16
ES2	Circular Uppercut	ES + m	17
ES3	Double Spin Kick	ES + j	16
ES4	Mountain Storm*	ES + h	22
ES5	Lightning Smash	ES + l + j	8-30
ES6	Tiger Spin Kick	ES + l + m	14-18
ES7	Tiger Frenzy	ES + h + j	10-15
ES8	Raging Tiger**	ES + h + m	9
	2nd hit		8
	3rd hit		7
	4th hit		6
	5th hit		6
	6th hit		6
	7th hit		20

*Throw

**All 7 hits are executed when the move is performed.

KOU'S STATUS UPGRADE BP COSTS

Status Raise	Life	Power	Defense
1-2	220	220	220
2-3	330	330	330
3-4	440	440	440
4-5	550	550	550
5-6	770	770	770
6-7	1100	1100	1100
7-8	1650	1650	1650

KOU'S EXTRA SKILLS BP COSTS

ES	Cost
Heel Smash	320
Circular Uppercut	400
Double Spin Kick	550
Mountain Storm	750
Lightning Smash	1000
Tiger Spin Kick	1200
Tiger Frenzy	1500
Raging Tiger	2500

KOU'S STATUS LEVELS

Status	Lv1	Lv2	Lv3	Lv4	Lv5	Lv6	Lv7	Lv8
Life	90	105	121	137	152	168	184	200
Power	60	77	95	113	131	149	167	185
Defense	70	90	110	130	150	170	190	210

BATTLE STRATEGIES

BATTLE 1

"Fate" Bar

Kou likes an easy night.

Dominique brightens things up.

Mikado agents storm the bar.

"<tch>... This Isn't Good!"

This first battle strategy will serve as a general introduction to Kou Leifoh's fighting technique and how to use it well. Some strategies and tips that are discussed in this section can be applied to *all* of Kou's fights. Other hints are more specific to this encounter.

RECOMMENDED CHOICE!

If you select Kou as the bouncer for the first fight, it can be difficult to score a lot of BP or even stay conscious. By choosing Kou, however, you get to hear the entire conversation Kou has on the phone in the event following the battle.

A quick study of Kou's list of combat moves shows that most of his moves just aren't all that powerful. When fighting as Kou, the player must use a great deal of patience and strategy, more so than with the other bouncers.

Kou's most powerful attacks include the Uppercut (h,H), the Heel Snap (m,M), and the Reverse Trip Kick (I,L). All of these combos begin with a light tap on the attack buttons. You should be able to execute Kou's full range of moves at the beginning of the game. Therefore, you must acquaint yourself with what exactly the difference is between a "light tap" and a "heavy tap."

LIGHT BUTTON TAP VS. HEAVY BUTTON TAP

To understand the difference between a "light tap" and a "heavy tap," go to the Sensitivity Configuration in the Options menu before starting a game. Scroll down to the Sensitivity controls for your controller. Leave the sensitivity at Medium, because it's the most flexible setting. Press the Square button, and the meter will measure the strength of your press. A "light tap" fills less than half the meter, and a "heavy tap" is any press that registers above half, no matter how quick.

The first battle pits the bouncers against five Mikado Special Forces (MSF) soldiers. Since the enemie are all quite a bit higher in Rank than Kou, he could very well get KO'd during this first battle. If he does get KO'd, this is the one time where the game will continue instead of ending when a character gets knocked out.

Kou starts the game with low stats in Power, Defense, and Life. Taking out all five enemies on your own in this first battle is quite difficult. When the enemy numbers dwindle, help your fellow bouncers and double-team the remaining stragglers.

Positioning is key. Make sure Kou is in the forefront of the fighting area, in a position where he's most visible. Always begin fighting from the outside, and then work your way inward. A good strategy to employ is to always make the enemy who is *in front of you* the top priority, and do everything to stay out of the middle, where enemies can often attack you from behind.

MSF have an evasive backflip that makes them hard to attack. Kou has a powerful move that propels him toward the enemy, called the Rolling [Ju]mp (j). Most of Kou's other moves knock enemies backward, but don't carry him forward. You can compensate for this by using this move.

[Kou] also has a Low attack move called the Slider (Direction + l), [bu]t it seems a bit more difficult to execute as compared to the [oth]er bouncers' directional moves. Generally, you want to yank [qui]ckly on the analog stick when attempting any of Kou's direc[tion]al moves, such as the Tiger Side Kick (Direction + j) or the [Dou]ble Side Kick (Direction + j (x2)).

There are enemies on the top and bottom levels, so after you KO the ones in the loft, run downstairs to finish off the MSF on the ground floor. Although the Spin Kick (J) is great at knocking down two or more enemies close together, the MSF tend to crouch so low that it rarely works. Instead, focus Kou's combination moves on one enemy until he goes down.

"THIS OUGHTA FINISH YOU OFF!"

With so many enemies in such tight quarters, the Trinity Rush attack will play a key role in this first battle. Just listen for Sion to say "Hey, c'mon!" When you hear this cue, press the R2 button to unleash the attack. While it looks like the trio teams up on one foe, actually *all* opponents are damaged in the attack.

Power Up!

The first BP Exchange screen appears after this fight. Since the MSF rank pretty well against you, you should receive 41 or 50 points for each enemy you take down.

After the battle, you will also receive Bonus Points dependent upon your overall Game Rank. Since you begin at Rank G, you will receive 100 points. Bonus Points received for battles will increase as your Game Rank improves.

Kou has the lowest exchange prices for Extra Skills, but the highest prices for status upgrades of all three bouncers. As you'll probably notice, Kou's lack of power serves as a downfall to take down enemies quickly enough to rack up the points.

[E]xchanging BP for status improvement is generally more important than purchasing Extra Skills. You should purchase a few status upgrades, and [th]en start buying Extra Skills to round out Kou's skills. This section will suggest when to buy Extra Skills for Kou.

[If] you do manage to gain enough BP in this first battle, begin by increasing Kou's Power level for 220 BP. If you can KO enemies more quickly, [th]en you can fight more enemies, score more points, and level up other stats faster.

BATTLE 2
Central Square

EVENT SEQUENCE

Dominique is captured by Mugetsu.

Kou gets chewed out.

He leads the bouncers to the MSD Cargo Train.

Guards block the entrance to the Station.

Surrounded

During this fight, you should concentrate on positioning Kou in a safe position. The MSF are lower in Rank this time and easier to fight, but th[e] bouncers are surrounded.

Use Kou's Rolling Stomp (j) attack on his first attacker. This should flatten the foe. Also, keep Kou positioned so that his bac[k] is to the gates. This should prevent hits from the back. While i[n] this position, use stationary moves such as the Triple Roundhou[se] Kick (H,h,h), Triple Jab (h,h,h), and Spinning Heel Drop (M).

You should also practice some of Kou's more damaging combination moves such as the Double Side Kick (Direction + j (x2)) and the Uppercut (h,H). Stay close to evasive MSF; if they backflip several times and get too far away, use the Rolling Stomp (j) to catch up.

Most of the battle occurs in the lower courtyard area, bu[t] you can also lead enemies t[o] the upper area. If by chance you can't find any enemies a[nd] the fight's still going on, che[ck] the upper courtyard area upstairs.

BATTLE 3
Central Station
EVENT SEQUENCE

A black panther seems to disturb Sion.

The station is heavily guarded.

The guards don't find Kou very charming.

Economy Class, Please

Finally, a battle where Kou might be able to KO *all* the enemies! The Mikado Security Guards are rather weak, thus making them the easiest to defea[t].

Because they remain mostly upright, they are susceptible to the full range of Kou's combat moves, including the Spin Kick (J) and Triple Roundhouse (H,h,h). However, using Kou's more difficult combination moves, such as Double Side Kick (Direction + j x2)) and the Heel Snap (m,M), will increase your chances of knocking out all three Guards yourself.

BATTLE 4
Central Station (Timed)

EVENT SEQUENCE

The MSD Cargo Train is ready to leave.

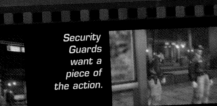

Security Guards want a piece of the action.

Kou explains that there's a time limit.

A Frenzied Fight

As Kou mentions, there is a time limit to this battle. You won't see a timer on-screen, and the whistle doesn't sound until the events following the battle. The fight will simply end after **45 seconds**.

If your characters KO all the enemies on-screen before the time limit, then the heroes get onboard the train. If not, then Sion will miss the train and struggle to catch up. It's almost worth it not to defeat all of the enemies here, since the cut-scene becomes more exciting!

At the start of the fight, steer Kou to the forefront of the cluster of enemies and attack a guy at the edge. If you knock him down before the enemy cluster spreads out, all the enemies will fall like dominoes! This is a great way to damage all foes at once.

Also, don't forget to use the Trinity Rush attack during this timed struggle if given the opportunity. Just because the battle is timed doesn't mean you can't unleash a flurry of hits with a Trinity Rush attack.

BATTLE 5
MSD Cargo Train

EVENT SEQUENCE

The bouncers stow away on the train.

Echidna dispatches her troops.

The bouncers hop into battle.

Protectors of the Cargo Train

During this fight, your character must duke it out for two rounds with two sets of three Security Guards. This provides a great opportunity to increase Kou's status and maybe even buy an Extra Skill. Keep this in mind, because the first Boss fight is upcoming.

Watch out for a wall of attacking Guards. To avoid getting flattened right away, perform Kou's Rolling Stomp move (j) about two steps from the Guards. If you hit one of them, chances are Kou will flatten all three instantly. If not, then Kou will at least sail to the rear of the platform, and they'll be surrounded! This means that the Guards will have their unprotected backs to each other, and you may be able to knock them all down when you take down one.

Power Up!

Your first Boss fight is coming up, so exchange BP for an Extra Skill this time instead of a status upgrade. Kou's Heel Smash (320 BP) will help out nicely in the fight to come.

BATTLE 6
Echidna (Boss) & Security Guards (2)

BOSS

ECHIDNA'S STATUS CHART

Status	Rank							
	G	F	E	D	C	B	A	S
Life	110	122	135	148	161	174	187	200
Power	80	93	107	120	134	147	161	175
Defense	90	106	122	139	155	172	188	205
BP	120	160	200	240	280	320	360	480

ECHIDNA'S EXTRA SKILLS

ES	Rank							
	G	F	E	D	C	B	A	S
Missile Kick	*	*	*	*	*	*	*	*
Cyclone Drive	-	*	*	*	*	*	*	*
Dead-End Carnival	-	-	*	*	*	*	*	*
Double Slap	-	-	-	*	*	*	*	*
Ambush Strike	-	-	-	-	*	*	*	*

You'd be such a hottie if only you kept your mouth shut!

Hottie with an Attitude

The bouncers are unceremoniously confronted by the leader of the pack on top of the speeding train. Needless to say, the Security Guards accompanying her are not a threat. You cannot, however, underestimate Echidna and her unique fighting style.

Make sure you raise your Guard at the start of the fight to avoid Echidna's initial attack, and then follow her attack with a Spinning Trip Kick (L). You must rely on this move and other Low attacks, because Echidna crouches down a lot during this fight and most other moves will sail over her head.

She is vulnerable to Low attacks, but Kou's Low attacks are not terribly powerful. Instead, unleash moves such as the Heel Snap (m,M) or the Extra Skill Heel Smash (ES + I). The Rolling Stomp (j) may also work, but not at close range. Be ready to block at all times, and make it a priority over attacking. It's possible to perform a Trinity Rush attack on Echidna, so use it.

Defeating Echidna will end the battle immediately, even if the Security Guards are still standing. The Security Guards don't pose much of a threat, so only focus on them if they get in the way. Of course, it adds to your total points if you can eliminate them. But if you try to engage a Guard and ignore Echidna, she may take advantage and try to attack from behind.

CARD KEY EVENT

After disposing of Echidna, an attack by a mysterious fighter-plane disables the train's brakes. You must find the Card Key or the train will crash into the station, causing the rocket fuel tanks to detonate.

Kou is the recommended choice for this scenario, because he provides more insight as to why the Cargo Train is being attacked, and by whom. Kou has 25 seconds to find the Card Key. Again, there is no timer displayed on-screen, so search quickly.

There are three boxes in the cab: one to the left, one to the right, and one on the floor by the doorway. Simply move Kou to any box to have him search it. The Card Key is always inside the last box you search. If you find it in time, the rocket fuel tanks will be disengaged and the train will simply crash into the station. However, if you're unsuccessful, the train will detonate upon impact and sea water will begin to flood the station.

This affects the next long battle, causing emergency shutters to close. The Game Over screen will appear if you get caught behind a shutter. The enemies encountered are also tougher, as explained in the next section, Battle 7.

Ugh! Leann... Can you say, "overkill"!?

Is this it?

BATTLE 7
Emergency Passage (Normal Scenario)

EVENT SEQUENCE

The rocket fuel tanks are released.

The bouncers escape the train.

Security Guards block the corridors.

A Minimum of Resistance

Getting through the emergency corridors is simple if you succeed in finding and using the Card Key onboard the MSD Cargo Train. There are four to five enemies on each floor, but in this case only three attack at the outset. The reinforcements will arrive shortly from the other section of the corridor, so make quick work of the first group.

EMERGENCY PASSAGE (NORMAL)
CARD KEY FOUND IN TIME

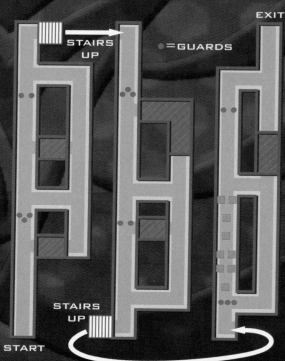

EXIT

STAIRS UP

● = GUARDS

STAIRS UP

START

The Security Chiefs are much tougher than the Security Guards. They are quicker to counterattack and more likely to block your moves. Since you must traverse three floors of enemies with only one full Life bar, you must be very cautious against the Security Chiefs, and use your Guard wisely.

If you don't neutralize the first wave of security before enemy backup arrives, simply listen for the audio cue from your fellow bouncer, and use a Trinity Rush attack to inflict major damage.

When the coast is clear (check the enemy status bar in the upper-right corner), run to the end of the corridor and up the stairs to the next level. For simple visual indicator, you can face a wall and look for a white arrow. These arrows point in the direction of the exit (or refer to the map). Also, here's no need to wait for slow comrades; they will be upstairs when the next round of battle starts. When you reach a big door marked "EXIT," run toward it to end the fight.

RECOMMENDED PATH!

Finding the Card Key and disconnecting the rocket fuel cars from the train in time make the battles in the Emergency Passage much easier. If you don't find the Card Key in time, then you must contend with more difficult enemies in greater numbers, plus you need to outrun closing emergency shutters and follow twisting corridors.

BATTLE 7
Emergency Passage (Closing Shutters Scenario)

EVENT SEQUENCE

u fails to find the Card Key.

The train destroys the station.

The corridors are flooded with sea water.

The emergency shutters are closing!

So You Couldn't Find the Card Key...

...or perhaps you **decided not to**, the latter reason the likely case. Because of this, the scenario in the MSD Station is different, with sea water flooding the entire area. This time, the emergency shutters are closing, and several sections of straightaway corridor are already sealed off.

The first battle is rather simple; however, concentrate your attacks on the Security Chief. You must eliminate all the enemies before proceeding. After the fight, Kou must run under a series of closing shutter doors before they completely close. This is easily accomplished by using the Analog Stick instead of the Directional Button.

EMERGENCY PASSAGE (ALTERNATE)
CARD KEY NOT FOUND IN TIME

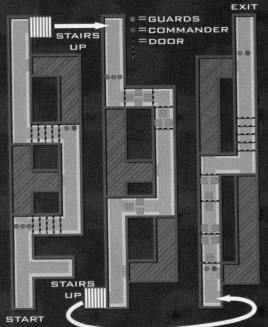

●= GUARDS
●= COMMANDER
▮= DOOR

EXIT

STAIRS UP

STAIRS UP

START

In the next area, you run into a Commander, an enemy unique to this alternate scenario. Commanders have advanced Defense and Power stats. They can also knock Kou to the ground with a shoulder-butt when given the opportunity.

To defeat Commanders, take them on with your entire team. Take out any minor enemies first (such as Security Guards), and then surround the Commander with your troops. Now you have a decided advantage.

Then it's time to outrun another corridor with closing shutters. Turn Kou to his right and continue down the corridor to the steps. In this scenario, proceed up two flights of steps and down a short stretch of hallway to catch up to your buddies.

The battle continues in this manner until you weave your way through the cargo containers on the 3rd floor and defeat all of the enemies. Be more cautious when facing the Commanders and Security Chiefs, and you should have no trouble racking up a lot of Bouncer Points. Use them to improve Kou's stats.

BATTLE 8
Air-Carrier

EVENT SEQUENCE

The Emergency Exit seems to be a dead end.

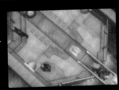
The area is littered with Air-Carriers.

The bouncers jump onto the carrier.

Commandeer an Air-Carrier!

The plan is to jump onboard a Mikado Air-Carrier, although it sounds extremely dangerous. The ship is full of Carrier Soldiers, some of the toughest in the Mikado organization. Your group is half-surrounded at the beginning of the match. Quickly raise your Guard at the outset to avoid getting knocked down.

...'t move Kou to the forefront immediately; you could potentially take a lot of damage along the way. Take out the nearest foe with Kou's Rolling ...mp (j), and then help double-team your comrade's opponent. If you can take out this second soldier quickly, then the bouncers are in prime ...e to easily take out the remaining Carrier Soldier.

...h Carrier Soldiers, the best strategy is to keep your Guard up ... let them perform one or two moves before retaliating. With ...h tight quarters, you can send an enemy flying with a move ...the Triple Roundhouse Kick (H,h,h) or the Heel Snap (m,M). ...'t forget to use a Trinity Rush attack if given the chance.

BATTLE 9
Hanging Garden

EVENT SEQUENCE

...e Air-
...er flies
...up the
...Mikado
...uilding.

The pilot
bails on the
bouncers.

The carrier
crashes
into the
Hanging
Garden.

Watchdogs
are alerted
to the
invasion.

Rocky Landing

...fter a rocky and noisy landing, some Watchdogs called "Bakilla" are alerted to the bouncers' presence. To make matters worse, MSF soldiers ...re dispatched to help eliminate the threat.

...ttack the closest Watchdog with a Slider (Direction + l) attack followed by several Reverse Trip Kick combos (l,L). Although not as dangerous ...s the MSF, the Watchdogs are a nuisance.

...se the same tactics discussed earlier when fighting MSF. Use the Uppercut (h,H) or Triple Roundhouse Kick (H,h,h) when they are in front of ...ou. If they backflip away, follow them with the Rolling Stomp (j) or the Slider.

Power Up!

...Kou's second Boss fight is at hand, so prepare him by purchasing another Extra Skill. If you have enough BP, purchase the Circular Uppercut. ...Kou gets surrounded several times in the following battle, no matter how hard you try to avoid it. This move strikes enemies both in front and ...ehind, making it very useful.

BATTLE 10

Mugetsu (Boss) & MSF Soldiers (4)

BOSS

MUGETSU W/MASK STATUS CHART

Status	Rank							
	G	F	E	D	C	B	A	S
Life	110	124	138	152	167	181	195	210
Power	90	105	121	137	152	168	184	200
Defense	70	84	98	112	127	141	155	170
BP	150	200	250	300	350	400	450	600

BOSS

MUGETSU W/MASK EXTRA SKILLS

ES	Rank							
	G	F	E	D	C	B	A	S
Ren-Getsu	-	-	✳	✳	✳	✳	✳	✳
Gen-Getsu (Hell)	✳	✳	✳	✳	✳	✳	✳	✳
Gen-Getsu (Heaven)	✳	✳	✳	✳	✳	✳	✳	✳
Hi-Getsu	-	-	-	-	✳	✳	✳	✳

The Psycho Man

Mugetsu arrives at the scene, and his sanity seems to be decaying at a rapid pace. He fights like a wild animal, taking on the nearest bouncer with reckless abandon. Don't allow Kou to become the focus of Mugetsu's rage, or he'll pound Kou repeatedly and follow him all over the combat area.

Fight the multiple MSF soldiers with the tactics you've used up to this point. Kou's strongest moves are the Uppercut (h,H) and the Heel Snap (m,M). If they backflip away, use the Rolling Stomp (j) or Slider (Direction + I) to narrow the gap.

If Mugetsu gets behind you and there's an MSF in front, perform Kou's Circular Uppercut (ES + m) over and over. This should knock Mugetsu away, and it will punish any MSF sneaking up from behind.

Mugetsu is resistant to Jump moves such as the Spin Kick and Tiger Side Kick, but the Double Side Kick (Direction + j ×2)) can catch him off-guard, especially with the second hit of the combo. Kou's Low attacks aren't very effective, and Mugetsu can easily block them. The only one worth using is the Slider (Direction + l), but only when Mugetsu is trying to be evasive.

Try out this cool trick, although the timing is crucial: knock down Mugetsu with a Heel Smash (ES + l) followed by the Rolling Stomp (j) while he's down.

BATTLE 11

Dauragon (Boss) & Black Panther

EVENT SEQUENCE

The bouncers perch outside the dome.

Dauragon faces off with Wong.

The arrogant villain underestimates the bouncers' skill.

ONE-ARMED DAURAGON'S STATUS CHART

Status	Rank							
	G	F	E	D	C	B	A	S
Life	120	134	148	162	177	191	205	220
Power	70	88	107	125	144	162	181	200
Defense	70	82	95	108	121	134	147	160
BP	110	146	183	220	256	293	330	440

ONE-ARMED DAURAGON'S EXTRA SKILLS

ES	Rank							
	G	F	E	D	C	B	A	S
Whirlwind Kick	*	*	*	*	*	*	*	*
Crescent Moon Slash	*	*	*	*	*	*	*	*
Triple Rave Kick	-	-	-	-	*	*	*	*
Elbow Spear	-	-	*	*	*	*	*	*

??? (BLACK PANTHER) STATUS CHART

Status	Rank							
	G	F	E	D	C	B	A	S
Life	100	113	127	140	154	167	181	195
Power	70	84	98	112	127	141	155	170
Defense	90	105	121	137	152	168	184	200
BP	120	160	200	240	280	320	360	480

The Mastermind of Mikado

Dauragon has a powerful spin kick that will knock down everyone, plus he follows it with a Reverse Sweep and a Double Talon Kick that keeps Kou on the ground. Also, you must keep a keen eye on the Black Panther circling the fighting arena.

Focus your attention on Dauragon. You should surround him, and do your best to keep him within your sights. When he turns his back to Kou, unleash the Heel Snap (m,M) or the Uppercut(h,H) for major damage. If Dauragon falls, follow up with the Rolling Stomp (j).

Dauragon's Guard is weak because of his self-imposed handicap, so long combo attacks like the Triple Jab (h,h,h) or Triple Roundhouse (H,h,h) will likely connect with at least one or two hits. You should avoid attacks like the Spin Kick or the Spinning Heel Drop. Dauragon often shows that he can counter your combo moves, right in the middle of your attempt!

If Dauragon constantly attacks Kou, back away as quickly as possible. Upon doing so, he should turn his attention back to the other bouncers. When the opportunity arises, hit him with a combo move like the Double Side Kick (Direction + j (x2)) or a Heel Smash (ES + I). The battle ends when Dauragon is defeated, regardless if the panther is still conscious.

Although it's best to concentrate on defeating Dauragon, you'll notice that the Black Panther is actually worth more BP than Dauragon. So if you want the extra BP, use Low attacks and in particular the Reverse Trip Kick (I,L). You can also cause damage with the Rolling Stomp (j).

BATTLE 18
MFB Room

The Inept Guard

Choosing Kou after the events following the fight with Dauragon means that he will be your choice to penetrate the Mikado Building. Although you'll have a chance to tally and exchange BP, you cannot select a different bouncer until Kou rejoins the others.

After a rather nasty fall, Kou is awakened by the stench of the Mikado Football Team's locker room. The lone MSF presents little challenge to Kou. Use powerful moves such as the Heel Snap (m,M) or the Uppercut (h,H) for some major damage. Wait until the soldier gets back up and repeat the process again.

Eww...
Smells like a sweat sock in here!

RECEIVED 33 BP!

MSF Society

Afterward, Kou dons the guard's outfit and leaves the cell. Outside, he notices how MSF greet each other. It's a type of security clearance procedure to uncover suspected impostors, so learn the moves fast or Kou will be found out!

The instructions are shown on-screen, so take a moment to practice them and study the frames. The only way this guide can help is by referring to specific posture signals.

Identify yourself!

If the wrong signal is given, it will almost always lead to a fight. The strategy for getting through is detailed in this section.

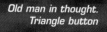
Old man in thought.
Triangle button

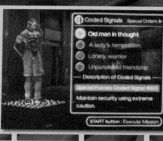

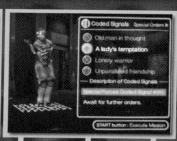

A lady's temptation.
Circle button

Lonely warrior. X button

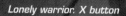

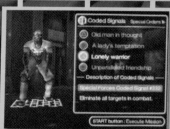

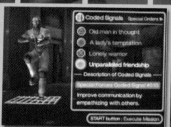

Unparalleled friendship.
Square button

Acing the Checkpoints

You'll find that the first series of encounters in the "Shopping Mall" are easy enough. Here's the breakdown of the MSF and their poses in the first section:

◎ **Check #1:** Random pose (either Square, Triangle, or Circle).

◎ **Check #2:** A pose not used in Check #1 is used here. For example, if the Triangle pose was used, then Square or Circle will be used here

◎ **Check #3:** The remaining pose *not* used during Checks #1 and #2 is used here.

If you fail any one of these tests, all three MSF will attack. Use a lot of anti-surround moves such as the Spin Kick (J), Triple Roundhouse (H,h,h), or the Circular Uppercut (ES + m) to get Kou out of trouble.

The next leg of Kou's undercover adventure is a bit trickier. The Guard at the entrance of the "Garden" takes Kou through a barrage of different poses. Here's how it works:

◎ **Check #4:** The MSF will throw every pose but the "Lonely warrior" at you. Striking the "Lonely warrior" pose will cause the MSF to attack you.

There are two ways to get by this checkpoint:

1. Enter the wrong pose (except for the "Lonely warrior") or take your time responding, and the Guard will send you down the right path.

2. Strike the correct pose each time, and you will proceed down the left path.

Check #5: If you fail at Check #4, the route shifts. This time, the "Lonely warrior" pose (X button) is the correct pose. Any other button press leads to a battle.

Check #6: You arrive at this checkpoint after clearing Check #4 or after finishing Check #5. This time, a MSF strikes poses too fast to imitate. The MSF is actually presenting a spinning roulette wheel of poses. Battle ensues if you incorrectly match the pose or if you press the X button.

Battles that break out in the Garden area are best fought on the narrower walkways, where the chances of Kou getting surrounded are less. Plus, when fighting on narrow stretches, you can knock down multiple MSFs with one attack if they get too close together.

The last section is a corridor full of MSF Elites, and it's quite a bit easier than the "Garden" area. It's broken down into two encounters:

Check #7: First, a lone Elite will approach Kou and nod. This time, Kou must decide the pose! Pick any one *except* the "Lonely warrior" (X button) and the Elite will copy Kou.

Check #8: Kou must copy two poses from Elite soldiers. The order in which you pose (for example, going left to right or right to left), is NOT important. If you fail, you must fight three MSF Elites and a P-101.

If Kou makes it through all three areas without being detected, he strikes the gallantly silly "superspy" pose. Bonus Points are still achieved even if no battles occur, with the amount dependent upon the player's overall Game Rank. The map below shows the locations at which all the Checks take place.

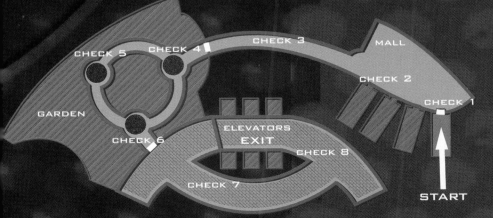

BATTLE 19

Mugetsu (Boss), MSF Soldiers (2), & MSF Elite (2)

EVENT SEQUENCE

Kou tries to fall in.

Sion is in hot water.

Kou crashes the party.

The bouncer team is together again.

BOSS

MUGETSU W/MASK STATUS CHART

Status	Rank							
	G	F	E	D	C	B	A	S
Life	110	124	138	152	167	181	195	210
Power	90	105	121	137	152	168	184	200
Defense	70	84	98	112	127	141	155	170
BP	150	200	250	300	350	400	450	600

BOSS

MUGETSU W/MASK EXTRA SKILLS

ES	Rank							
	G	F	E	D	C	B	A	S
Ren-Getsu	-	-	*	*	*	*	*	*
Gen-Getsu (Hell)	*	*	*	*	*	*	*	*
Gen-Getsu (Heaven)	*	*	*	*	*	*	*	*
Hi-Getsu	-	-	-	-	*	*	*	*

A Trap Backfires

Blending in with a cadre of MSF, Kou finds himself in the executive office as Sion gets ambushed by Mugetsu. While Kou circles the area to get closer to Dominique, Volt enters and finds a new use for Kou. After Kou recovers, it's time to show Mugetsu that his last defeat wasn't just a fluke!

Like the previous encounter with Mugetsu at the Hanging Garden, use a roaming-fighting method. At the start, focus your attention on the MSF and Elite soldiers, using the same tactics used previously. Use the Triple Roundhouse (H,h,h) and the Heel Snap (m,M) on MSF within close range.

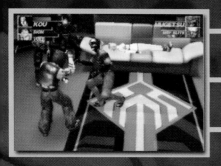

Keep Kou out of the center of the fighting area, and place his back against a wall. When Mugetsu draws near while Kou is fighting an MSF, do a move that will knock down your current foe and then turn your attention to Mugetsu. Since Mugetsu moves around a lot, Kou may get drawn into a small crowd and surrounded. This is the time to use moves such as the Circular Uppercut (ES + m) or the Spin Kick (J) to take down enemies in all directions.

Use a Trinity Rush attack whenever possible. It's helpful to get all the MSF and Elite enemies out of the way so that you can focus on defeating Mugetsu. It doesn't hurt to damage Mugetsu several times with a Trinity Rush attack either.

Against Mugetsu, focus on using damaging moves such as the Uppercut (h,H) and the Heel Snap (m,M). The Boss is resistant to Jump moves like the Spin Kick; however, the Double Side Kick (Direction + j (x2)) can be effective, especially with the second hit of the combo. The battle ends when Mugetsu gets KO'd, regardless of the status of the other enemies.

BATTLE 20
Rocket Tower 6F to 2F

EVENT SEQUENCE

Dominique is revived.

The Rocket Tower goes on full alert.

The team decides to split up.

Dominique isn't happy to be stuck with Kou.

The Robot Horde

While Dominique would be happier if Sion led her through the perils of the Rocket Tower, Kou will prove his worth in the long and difficult fight ahead. The bouncer chosen to protect Dominique must survive a multi-level gauntlet of robot sentinels. Keep in mind the following conditions:

- You must survive all levels with only one Life bar; no breaks or refills.

- Dominique must also survive all levels with only one Life bar. If she gets KO'd before the final exit, it's "Game Over."

- If Kou's or Dominique's Life bars get down to 25% or less, you'd best stop fighting the robots and run directly to the final exit.

- When fighting the robots, you should choose single, non-combo moves that you can quickly repeat. Avoid using moves that take a long time for Kou to recover his fighting stance. The robots *will retaliate* in between your attacks.

Characters with higher Ranks are better suited to take on every robot and enemy in the Rocket Tower. But as a beginner at F or E Rank (estimated), you must pick and choose your battles wisely. This section provides pointers on who to fight, who not to fight, and how to survive.

You first encounter a couple of orange robots called LD-15s. At this point, you're better off running over to the side wall and leading Dominique all the way around the platform to the exit stairs.

The P-101 is difficult to fight, since Kou's Middle and Low attacks lack killing power. The smaller robot runs interference for the heavy load lifters.

On the next level, you encounter a gray, humanoid robot called an MC-07. Use the Triple Jab (h,h,h) to knock it back, and then fly in close with the Rolling Stomp (j). Like most robots, you can interrupt the MC-07's attacks with your own.

As you're fighting the MC-07, beware of an LD-15 approaching from the rear. If the MC-07 is knocked behind the LD-15 by your blows, then turn Kou to face the larger worker droid and focus your assault on it. Just avoid getting surrounded. Against LD-15s, use Kou's Rolling Stomp (j) repeatedly. Proceed up the stairs to take on another MC-07, and then descend the next set of stairs and take out the next LD-15 in front of the exit.

On the 4th floor, you're treated to the lowly Security Guard. Use similar tactics discussed earlier. As you proceed, you'll encounter some MC-07s. If you're at a low Rank, you may want to avoid this fight.

Down the stairs, a Security Chief will engage Kou. Keep your Guard up until he attacks, and then retaliate with a powerful move like Triple Roundhouse (H,h,h) or the Uppercut (h,H). If you knock him down the stairs, pursue him all the way down and nail him again when he gets back up.

Once you reach Level 3, look for two bridge structures that connect to the next platform. An LD-15 blocks the right bridge. Lead Dominique toward the MC-07 and dispose of it, but be warned that another MC-07 and a big LD-15 are moving in all the while.

...her set of dual bridges will take you to ...ext platform. You can avoid confronta-...with the LD-15 and the MC-07 alto-...er by crossing on the left-hand bridge. ...e left of their position is the stairwell ... to the final level.

...u move Kou straight ahead from the bottom of the steps, you'll encounter a lone MC-07 that is easy to take out. Beyond it is the green-...red lift marking the exit. Depending on how much Life you have at this point, you may want to engage the MC-07 and the LD-15 located ...he other side for extra Bouncer Points.

BATTLE 21

PD-4 (Boss)

PD-4'S STATUS CHART

Status	Rank							
	G	F	E	D	C	B	A	S
Life	120	134	148	162	177	191	205	220
Power	90	102	115	128	141	154	167	180
Defense	95	107	120	133	146	159	172	185
BP	170	226	283	340	396	453	510	680

PD-4'S EXTRA SKILLS

Skill Name	Rank							
	G	F	E	D	C	B	A	S
Thunder Fall	-	-	*	*	*	*	*	*
Lightning Whip	*	*	*	*	*	*	*	*
Elbow Spin Break	*	*	*	*	*	*	*	*
Lightning Viper	-	-	-	-	*	*	*	*

The Superweapon Redefined

Kou and Dominique run into PD-4 on the lowest level of the Rocket Tower. While it has been ordered to retrieve Dominique, Sion and Volt arrive to help Kou prevent anything from happening.

Three on one...
Those are acceptable odds...

From the outset, raise Kou's Guard and deflect PD-4's [ini]tial attack. After unleashing a long, multi-hit combo, how[ev]er, PD-4 needs a moment to recover its center of bala[nce]. Once you see an opening, unleash Kou's Double Side Ki[ck] (Direction + j (x2)), the Uppercut (h,H), and the Heel S[?] (m,M).

Try to surround your bouncers around PD-4, so that it has trouble deciding which side to attack and block. Essentially, PD-4 isn't very difficult. You must be patient and guard against the enemy's long combo attacks, waiting for the proper moment to strike back.

You should also use a Trinity Rush attack whenever possible. There should be several opportunities, since you'll probably spend most of the fight standing there with your Guard up.

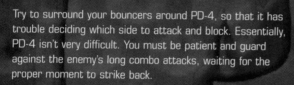

BATTLE 22
Rocket Tower—Basement

EVENT SEQUENCE

The irre-pressible Mugetsu steals Dominique again.

You bastard, you're still alive...!?

Sion resolves to save Dominique.

The LD-X1 debuts.

Stay on your toes, Sion!

he New Model Loader

black loader robot is slightly stronger and has a longer Life bar than the other two. Take out the LD-15s first using Kou's Rolling Stomp (j).
LD-X1 is a bit nastier, but Kou's Rolling Stomp trick still applies.

ower Up!

time to expand Kou's repertoire of moves once more, to prepare him for the upcoming Boss fights. When your BP and Bonus Points are
lied up this time, purchase Kou's Double Spin Kick move (550 BP) if possible.

BATTLE 23

Echidna (Boss) & LD-X1 Robots (2)

ECHIDNA'S STATUS CHART

Status	Rank							
	G	F	E	D	C	B	A	S
Life	110	122	135	148	161	174	187	200
Power	80	93	107	120	134	147	161	175
Defense	90	106	122	139	155	172	188	205
BP	120	160	200	240	280	320	360	480

ECHIDNA'S EXTRA SKILLS

ES	Rank							
	G	F	E	D	C	B	A	S
Missile Kick	✳	✳	✳	✳	✳	✳	✳	✳
Cyclone Drive	-	✳	✳	✳	✳	✳	✳	✳
Dead-End Carnival	-	-	✳	✳	✳	✳	✳	✳
Double Slap	-	-	-	✳	✳	✳	✳	✳
Ambush Strike	-	-	-	-	✳	✳	✳	✳

Once I defeat all of YOU!

Hell Hath No Fury...

The red-headed vixen has returned! This time, she's brought better backup support in the form of two
LD-X1s. These robotic menaces are like giant moving walls.

Just like in the previous fight, you should guard
mmediately to counter Echidna's spinning fight-
r moves. As she attempts to get up, nail her
with a Spinning Trip Kick (L) followed instantly by
a Rolling Stomp (j). When performed correctly,
you will knock her to the ground and hit her
again while she is down.

It's not a bad idea to go after a machine and keep hitting it over and over with Kou's Rolling Stomp move (j). This pushes the robot across the room and breaks up the cluster of enemies, which can be a deadly formation.

Since Echidna hovers close to the ground, rely on moves like the Reverse Trip Kick (l,L) and perhaps the Heel Snap combo (m,M). That's why we suggested that Kou learn the Double Spin Kick (ES + j) after the last battle. That move adds another powerful move to use against her. The Heel Smash (ES + l) is also effective at knocking her to the floor.

Lastly, use a Trinity Rush attack whenever the audio cue arises. Always remember to press the R1 button whenever Echidna dives for the floor to block her foot frenzy.

BATTLE 24
Mugetsu (Boss)

BOSS

MUGETSU W/O MASK STATUS CHART

Status	Rank							
	G	F	E	D	C	B	A	S
Life	120	134	148	162	177	191	205	220
Power	100	115	131	147	162	178	194	210
Defense	65	79	93	107	122	136	150	165
BP	180	240	300	360	420	480	540	720

BOSS

MUGETSU W/O MASK EXTRA SKILLS

Name	Rank							
	G	F	E	D	C	B	A	S
Shi-Getsu	-	*	*	*	*	*	*	*
Fuku-Getsu	-	-	-	-	*	*	*	*
Ka-Getsu	-	-	*	*	*	*	*	*
Ren-Getsu	*	*	*	*	*	*	*	*

EVENT SEQUENCE

The Galeos launches.

Leann gives Kou a plan.

The bouncers grab a ride.

Mugetsu botches up your landing!

The Return of Psycho Boy!

ou's plan to get onboard the Galeos shuttle with the Air-Carrier is a bit risky, and everything seems to go fine until Mugetsu steps in again! This me around, you'll discover that he is a much more lethal opponent than in previous battles. You must first decide, "Who's going to fly the carri- ?" Since this strategy is for Kou, it's obvious that you don't want him piloting the craft.

aise your Guard and wait for Mugetsu to attack. He will most likely perform a Crazy Drill, where he instantly becomes horizontal and fires him- elf like a torpedo. As Mugetsu recovers from this attack, unleash an Uppercut (h,H) and then move so that Mugetsu is between you and your artner. If he goes after your partner, attack him from the rear. If not, raise your Guard and wait for him to attack again, and then perform nother strong combo move like the Heel Snap (m,M) or Double Side Kick (Direction + j (x2)).

Since there are only two bouncers in this battle, you can't use a Trinity Rush attack. Also, you don't want to let your partner get KO'd. Taking on Mugetsu with only one bouncer can prove to be a difficult task. You need a fellow bouncer to distract Mugetsu occasionally, so that you can hit him from the back side.

Beware of Mugetsu's Ren-Getsu move, one in which he begins to spin like a top above the ground. If he does this in front of Kou, keep your Guard up the whole time. Kou can constantly perform the Spinning Trip Kick (L) on Mugetsu. However, since the attack isn't very powerful, winning the battle could take a long time.

BATTLE 25
Black Panther (Sub-Boss)

BOSS

BLACK PANTHER'S STATUS CHART

Status	Rank							
	G	F	E	D	C	B	A	S
Life	100	113	127	140	154	167	181	195
Power	70	84	98	112	127	141	155	170
Defense	90	105	121	137	152	168	184	200
BP	120	160	200	240	280	320	360	480

BOSS

BLACK PANTHER'S EXTRA SKILLS

ES	Rank							
	G	F	E	D	C	B	A	S
Griffin Talons	-	-	*	*	*	*	*	*
Meteor Storm	*	*	*	*	*	*	*	*
Griffin Tail	-	-	-	-	*	*	*	*
Spinning Rush	*	*	*	*	*	*	*	*
Wild Fang	-	-	-	*	*	*	*	*
Shape Shift	*	*	*	*	*	*	*	*

Beautiful Stranger

Onboard the Galeos, the mysterious Black Panther looks to keep the bouncers from reaching the control room. I guess the bouncers will just have to fight their way through.

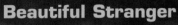

Hey, it's that black panther again!

...ce the panther is low to the ground, Low attacks are the ...y to go. Also note that the Black Panther can counter Kou's ...w attack combos. This limits you to the Spinning Trip Kick (L), ...ch works regularly but prolongs the battle. The Heel Smash ...5 + l) also deals lethal damage to the beast. A growl from ... beast indicates that it's about to attack, so make sure your ...ard is up.

When the Black Panther shape-shifts into human female form, knock her to the ground with a combo such as the Heel Snap (m,M) or the Triple Roundhouse (H,h,h).

BATTLE 26
Dauragon II (Boss)

BOSS

DAURAGON'S STATUS CHART

Status	Rank							
	G	F	E	D	C	B	A	S
Life	125	140	155	170	185	200	215	230
Power	80	97	114	131	148	165	182	200
Defense	80	94	108	122	137	151	165	180
BP	150	200	250	300	350	400	450	600

DAURAGON'S EXTRA SKILLS

Name	Rank							
	G	F	E	D	C	B	A	S
Whirlwind Kick	*	*	*	*	*	*	*	*
Crescent Moon Slash	*	*	*	*	*	*	*	*
Dragon Claw	-	-	*	*	*	*	*	*
Dragon Blitz	*	*	*	*	*	*	*	*
Wyvern's Sting	-	-	-	-	*	*	*	*

King of Fighters

...or the Dauragon Boss fight, your bouncer must fight *two* rounds in which there is no opportunity ...etween fights to select a different bouncer. In addition, your bouncer's Life bar will not refill between ...attles. This battle will put your Defense meter to work. If Kou loses the ability to block, Dauragon will ...ake quick work of him.

The fighting area in the Galeos is ample, but you should avoid the curved areas to the left and right of Dominique's position. Resorting to those areas makes it difficult to implement the following strategy.

Immediately surround Dauragon at the start of the fight. Once he is surrounded, keep your Guard up until he turns his back to you and then execute a fierce combo attack to his rear.

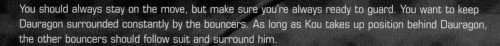

You should always stay on the move, but make sure you're always ready to guard. You want to keep Dauragon surrounded constantly by the bouncers. As long as Kou takes up position behind Dauragon, the other bouncers should follow suit and surround him.

With bouncers on all sides, Dauragon will attack and defend in all different directions. He even has a spinning kick that can knock down everyone at once.

Dauragon is very quick and can even block rear attacks. With Dauragon in front of you with his Guard up, perform a three-move combo attack like the Triple Jab (h,h,h) or Triple Roundhouse Kick (H,h,h). This may cause Dauragon to drop his Guard, enabling the last and most powerful punch to connect. Also, avoid moves that involve jumping, spinning, or sweeping the ground.

Keep in mind that a Trinity Rush attack will NOT work against Dauragon. He simply fights his way out of it before it can be executed. If Dauragon constantly attacks your Guard, back away until he turns his back and focuses on the others.

You must fight this battle smartly. You should finish off Dauragon and still have 50% or more of your Life and Defense intact. If not, it's unlikely you'll survive the next round.

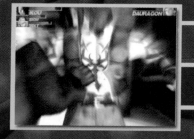

Power Up!

Although you can't save or switch bouncers between battles, you do receive a chance to exchange BP. You should wisely spend whatever Bouncer Points you have accumulated from the last fight.

If you have enough for an Extra Skill, then purchase Kou's Double Spin Kick (550 BP). This attack is extremely useful in countering Dauragon, especially while he is attempting to guard himself. While the Tiger Spin Kick is a lightning-quick series of furious footwork and is extremely useful in countering Dauragon in mid-attack, the player will probably not amass enough BP to purchase it during the first game.

If you can't purchase an Extra Skill, then improve Kou's Power level. Spending BP on Defense or Life will lengthen the meter, but the player **will not recover** lost Life or Defense by upgrading either of these.

BATTLE 27
Dauragon III (Boss)

DAURAGON (OVERALLS) STATUS CHART

Status	Rank							
	G	F	E	D	C	B	A	S
Life	130	145	160	175	190	205	220	235
Power	100	114	128	142	157	171	185	200
Defense	100	112	125	138	151	164	177	190
BP	220	293	366	440	513	586	660	880

DAURAGON (OVERALLS) EXTRA SKILLS

Name	Rank							
	G	F	E	D	C	B	A	S
Sonic Elbow	*	*	*	*	*	*	*	*
Dragon Spiral	*	*	*	*	*	*	*	*
Launcher	-	-	*	*	*	*	*	*
Jet Uppercut	-	-	-	-	*	*	*	*

The Desperate Hour

In round two, Dauragon moves more quickly and attacks more frequently. Once again, have your bouncers surround Dauragon from the start and use Kou's Double Side Kick move (Direction + j (x2)) when there's an opening.

As was the case in the first fight, you must keep moving and ensure your bouncers encircle Dauragon. However, this proves more difficult because of his unblockable Extra Skill Jet Uppercut.

With Dauragon defeated, the game isn't quite over. The Ending Event Sequence depends on which bouncer you chose for certain battles and certain scenarios in the game. There is a section in the "Secrets" at the end of this chapter that explains how the endings play out.

During Kou's Epilogue, there may be one last fight that occurs with a hidden character. Check out the section called "Secrets" for further details.

Sorry, I know you're closing shop soon, but I've got one more job for you.

STORY MODE APPENDIX

The following section contains a rundown of every enemy encounter in the game, and lists each enemy's strength distribution chart. Use this as a reference before heading into battle.

ENEMY STRENGTH DISTRIBUTION CHARTS

Battle 1: "FATE" Bar

ENEMY STRENGTH DISTRIBUTION CHART

Enemy	G	F	E	D	C	B	A	S
MSF	E	E	E	D	D	C	C	B
MSF	E	E	D	D	C	C	B	B
MSF	E	E	D	D	C	C	B	B
MSF	D	D	D	C	C	B	A	A
MSF	D	D	C	C	B	B	A	A

Battle 2: Central Square

ENEMY STRENGTH DISTRIBUTION CHART

Enemy	G	F	E	D	C	B	A	S
MSF	G	G	F	E	D	C	C	B
MSF	G	G	F	E	D	C	C	B
MSF	G	F	E	D	D	C	B	A
MSF	F	E	D	D	C	C	B	A
MSF	F	E	D	D	C	B	A	

Battle 3: Central Station

ENEMY STRENGTH DISTRIBUTION CHART

Enemy	G	F	E	D	C	B	A	S
SECURITY GUARD	G	G	F	E	D	C	C	B
SECURITY GUARD	G	G	F	E	D	C	C	B
SECURITY GUARD	G	F	E	D	D	C	B	A

Battle 4: Central Station (Timed)

ENEMY STRENGTH DISTRIBUTION CHART

Enemy	G	F	E	D	C	B	A	S
SECURITY GUARD	G	G	F	E	D	C	C	B
SECURITY GUARD	G	G	F	E	D	C	C	B
SECURITY GUARD	G	F	E	D	D	C	B	A
SECURITY GUARD	G	F	E	D	D	C	B	A
SECURITY GUARD	F	E	D	D	C	C	B	A

Battle 5: MSD Cargo Train

ENEMY STRENGTH DISTRIBUTION CHART—ROUND 1

Enemy	G	F	E	D	C	B	A	S
SECURITY GUARD	G	G	F	E	D	C	C	B
SECURITY GUARD	G	F	E	D	D	C	B	A
SECURITY GUARD	G	F	E	D	D	C	B	A

Battle 5: Continued

ENEMY STRENGTH DISTRIBUTION CHART—ROUND 2

Enemy	G	F	E	D	C	B	A	S
SECURITY GUARD	G	G	F	E	D	C	C	B
SECURITY GUARD	G	F	E	D	D	C	B	A
SECURITY GUARD	F	E	D	D	C	C	B	A

Battle 6: Echidna (Boss) & Security Guards (2)

ENEMY STRENGTH DISTRIBUTION CHART

Enemy	G	F	E	D	C	B	A	S
ECHIDNA	G	F	E	D	C	B	A	S
SECURITY GUARD	G	G	F	E	D	C	C	B
SECURITY GUARD	F	E	D	D	C	C	B	A

Battle 7: Emergency Passage (Normal Scenario)

EMERGENCY PASSAGE: OPEN SHUTTER—1F

Enemy	G	F	E	D	C	B	A	S
SECURITY CHIEF	G	G	F	E	D	C	C	B
SECURITY CHIEF	G	F	E	D	D	C	B	A
SECURITY GUARD	G	G	F	E	D	C	C	B
SECURITY GUARD	G	F	E	D	D	C	B	A
SECURITY GUARD	G	F	E	D	D	C	B	A

EMERGENCY PASSAGE: OPEN SHUTTER—2F

Enemy	G	F	E	D	C	B	A	S
SECURITY CHIEF	G	G	F	E	D	C	C	B
SECURITY GUARD	G	G	F	E	D	C	C	B
SECURITY GUARD	G	F	E	D	D	C	B	A
SECURITY GUARD	F	E	D	D	C	C	B	A
SECURITY GUARD	F	E	D	D	C	B	A	

EMERGENCY PASSAGE: OPEN SHUTTER—3F

Enemy	G	F	E	D	C	B	A	S
SECURITY CHIEF	G	G	F	E	D	C	C	B
SECURITY CHIEF	G	F	E	D	D	C	B	A
SECURITY GUARD	G	F	E	D	D	C	B	A
SECURITY GUARD	F	E	D	D	C	C	B	A

Battle 7: Emergency Passage (Closing Shutters Scenario)

EMERGENCY PASSAGE: CLOSING SHUTTER—1F

Enemy	G	F	E	D	C	B	A	S
SECURITY CHIEF	G	G	F	E	D	C	C	B
SECURITY GUARD	G	F	E	D	D	C	B	A
SECURITY GUARD	G	F	E	D	D	C	B	A

EMERGENCY PASSAGE: CLOSING SHUTTER—1F-B

Enemy	G	F	E	D	C	B	A	S
COMMANDER	G	G	F	E	D	C	C	B
SECURITY GUARD	G	G	F	E	D	C	C	B

EMERGENCY PASSAGE: CLOSING SHUTTER—2F-A

Enemy	G	F	E	D	C	B	A	S
SECURITY CHIEF	G	F	E	D	D	C	B	A
SECURITY GUARD	G	G	F	E	D	C	C	B
SECURITY GUARD	F	E	D	D	C	B	A	

EMERGENCY PASSAGE: CLOSING SHUTTER - 3F-B

Enemy	G	F	E	D	C	B	A	S
COMMANDER	G	G	F	E	D	C	C	B
SECURITY GUARD	G	F	E	D	D	C	B	A

EMERGENCY PASSAGE: CLOSING SHUTTER - 4F

Enemy	G	F	E	D	C	B	A	S
COMMANDER	G	F	E	D	D	C	B	A
SECURITY GUARD	G	F	E	D	D	C	B	A

Battle 8: Air-Carrier

ENEMY STRENGTH DISTRIBUTION CHART

Enemy	G	F	E	D	C	B	A	S
CARRIER SOLDIER	G	G	F	E	D	C	C	B
CARRIER SOLDIER	G	F	E	D	D	C	B	A
CARRIER SOLDIER	F	E	D	D	C	B	A	

Battle 9: Hanging Garden

ENEMY STRENGTH DISTRIBUTION CHART

Enemy	G	F	E	D	C	B	A	S
MSF	E	E	D	C	C	B	B	A
MSF	F	E	D	D	C	C	B	A
MSF	G	G	F	E	D	C	C	B
WATCHDOG	G	G	F	E	D	C	C	B
WATCHDOG	F	E	D	D	C	B	A	

Battle 10: Mugetsu (Boss) & MSF Soldiers (4)

ENEMY STRENGTH DISTRIBUTION CHART

Enemy	G	F	E	D	C	B	A	S
MUGETSU (W/MASK)	G	F	E	D	C	B	A	S
MSF	E	E	D	C	C	B	B	A
MSF	F	E	D	D	C	C	B	A
MSF	G	F	E	D	D	C	B	A
MSF	G	G	F	E	D	C	C	B

Battle 11: Dauragon (Boss) & Black Panther

ENEMY STRENGTH DISTRIBUTION CHART

Enemy	G	F	E	D	C	B	A	S
DAURAGON (1-ARMED)	G	F	E	D	C	B	A	S
??? (PANTHER)	G	F	E	D	C	B	A	S

Battle 12: Mikado Building—65F Hall

ENEMY STRENGTH DISTRIBUTION CHART

Enemy	G	F	E	D	C	B	A	S
SECURITY GUARD	G	G	F	E	D	C	C	B
SECURITY GUARD	G	F	E	D	D	C	B	A

Surprise Battle: Mikado Building—65F Elevators

ENEMY STRENGTH DISTRIBUTION CHART

Enemy	G	F	E	D	C	B	A	S
MSF	G	G	F	E	D	C	C	B
MSF	G	G	F	E	D	C	C	B
MSF	G	F	E	D	D	C	B	A
MSF	F	E	D	D	C	C	B	A

Surprise Battle: Mikado Building—65F Conference Room

ENEMY STRENGTH DISTRIBUTION CHART

Enemy	G	F	E	D	C	B	A	S
COMMANDER	G	F	E	D	D	C	B	A
P-101	G	G	F	E	D	C	C	B

Battle 13: Mikado Building—66F Hall

ENEMY STRENGTH DISTRIBUTION CHART

Enemy	Game Rank vs. Enemy Rank							
	G	F	E	D	C	B	A	S
P-101	G	G	F	E	D	C	C	B
P-101	G	F	E	D	D	C	B	A
SECURITY GUARD	G	G	F	E	D	C	C	B
SECURITY GUARD	G	F	E	D	D	C	B	A
SECURITY GUARD	F	E	D	D	C	C	B	A
SECURITY GUARD	E	E	D	C	C	B	B	A

Battle 14: Mikado Building—Data Room

ENEMY STRENGTH DISTRIBUTION CHART

Enemy	Game Rank vs. Enemy Rank							
	G	F	E	D	C	B	A	S
MSF ELITE	G	G	F	E	D	C	C	B
MSF	G	F	E	D	D	C	B	A

Battle 15: Black Panther (Sub-Boss)

ENEMY STRENGTH DISTRIBUTION CHART

Enemy	Game Rank vs. Enemy Rank							
	G	F	E	D	C	B	A	S
??? (PANTHER)	G	F	E	D	C	B	A	S

Battle 16: Mikado Building—Enhancement Surgery Area

ENEMY STRENGTH DISTRIBUTION CHART

Enemy	Game Rank vs. Enemy Rank							
	G	F	E	D	C	B	A	S
MSF	G	G	F	E	D	C	C	B
MSF	G	F	E	D	D	C	B	A

Battle 17: Mikado Building—Bio-Plant/Robot Factory

BIO-PLANT

Enemy	Game Rank vs. Enemy Rank							
	G	F	E	D	C	B	A	S
MSF ELITE	G	G	F	E	D	C	C	B
P-101	G	G	F	E	D	C	C	B
P-101	G	F	E	D	D	C	B	A
MSF	G	F	E	D	D	C	B	A
MSF	G	F	E	D	D	C	B	A

ROBOT FACTORY

Enemy	Game Rank vs. Enemy Rank							
	G	F	E	D	C	B	A	S
MSF ELITE	G	G	F	E	D	C	C	B
MSF ELITE	G	F	E	D	D	C	B	A
MSF ELITE	G	F	E	D	D	C	B	A
MSF	G	G	F	E	D	C	C	B
MSF	G	G	F	E	D	C	C	B
MSF	G	F	E	D	D	C	B	A
MSF	F	E	D	D	C	C	B	A

Battle 18: MFB Room

ENEMY STRENGTH DISTRIBUTION CHART

Enemy	Game Rank vs. Enemy Rank							
	G	F	E	D	C	B	A	S
MSF	G	F	E	D	D	C	B	A

Battle 19: Mugetsu (Boss), MSF Soldiers (2), & MSF Elite (2)

ENEMY STRENGTH DISTRIBUTION CHART

Enemy	Game Rank vs. Enemy Rank							
	G	F	E	D	C	B	A	S
MUGETSU (W/MASK)	G	F	E	D	C	B	A	S
MSF ELITE	G	F	E	D	D	C	B	A
MSF ELITE	F	E	D	D	C	C	B	A
MSF	F	E	D	D	C	C	B	A
MSF	E	E	D	C	C	B	B	A

Battle 20: Rocket Tower 6F to 2F

ROCKET TOWER: 6F

Enemy	Game Rank vs. Enemy Rank							
	G	F	E	D	C	B	A	S
LD-15	G	G	F	E	D	C	C	B
LD-15	G	G	F	E	D	C	C	B
P-101	F	E	D	D	C	C	B	A

ROCKET TOWER: 5F

Enemy	Game Rank vs. Enemy Rank							
	G	F	E	D	C	B	A	S
LD-15	G	G	F	E	D	C	C	B
LD-15	G	F	E	D	D	C	B	A
MC-07	G	G	F	E	D	C	C	B
MC-07	G	G	F	E	D	C	C	B

ROCKET TOWER: 4F

Enemy	Game Rank vs. Enemy Rank							
	G	F	E	D	C	B	A	S
SECURITY CHIEF	E	E	D	C	C	B	B	A
SECURITY CHIEF	E	E	D	C	C	B	B	A
MC-07	G	G	F	E	D	C	C	B
MC-07	G	F	E	D	D	C	B	A

ROCKET TOWER: 3F

Enemy	Game Rank vs. Enemy Rank							
	G	F	E	D	C	B	A	S
LD-15	G	G	F	E	D	C	C	B
LD-15	G	F	E	D	D	C	B	A
LD-15	G	F	E	D	D	C	B	A
MC-07	G	F	E	D	D	C	B	A
MC-07	G	F	E	D	D	C	B	A
MC-07	F	E	D	D	C	C	B	A

ROCKET TOWER: 2F

Enemy	Game Rank vs. Enemy Rank							
	G	F	E	D	C	B	A	S
LD-15	F	E	D	D	C	B	A	
MC-07	F	E	D	D	C	C	B	A
MC-07	E	E	D	C	C	B	B	A

Battle 21: PD-4 (Boss)

ENEMY STRENGTH DISTRIBUTION CHART

Enemy	Game Rank vs. Enemy Rank								
	G	F	E	D	C	B	A	S
PD-4	G	F	E	D	C	B	A	S

Battle 22: Rocket Tower—Basement

ENEMY STRENGTH DISTRIBUTION CHART

Enemy	Game Rank vs. Enemy Rank								
	G	F	E	D	C	B	A	S
LD-X1	G	G	F	E	D	C	C	B
LD-15	F	E	D	D	C	C	B	A
LD-15	E	E	D	C	C	B	B	A

Battle 23: Echidna (Boss) & LD-X1 Robots (x2)

ENEMY STRENGTH DISTRIBUTION CHART

Enemy	Game Rank vs. Enemy Rank								
	G	F	E	D	C	B	A	S
ECHIDNA	G	F	E	D	C	B	A	S
LD-X1	F	E	D	D	C	C	B	A
LD-X1	F	E	D	D	C	C	B	A

Battle 24: Mugetsu (Boss)

ENEMY STRENGTH DISTRIBUTION CHART

Enemy	Game Rank vs. Enemy Rank								
	G	F	E	D	C	B	A	S
MUGETSU (W/O MASK)	G	F	E	D	C	B	A	S

Battle 25: Black Panther (Sub-Boss)

ENEMY STRENGTH DISTRIBUTION CHART

Enemy	Game Rank vs. Enemy Rank								
	G	F	E	D	C	B	A	S
??? (PANTHER)	G	F	E	D	C	B	A	S

Battle 26: Dauragon II (Boss)

ENEMY STRENGTH DISTRIBUTION CHART

Enemy	Game Rank vs. Enemy Rank								
	G	F	E	D	C	B	A	S
DAURAGON (NORMAL)	G	F	E	D	C	B	A	S

Battle 27: Dauragon III (Boss)

ENEMY STRENGTH DISTRIBUTION CHART

Enemy	Game Rank vs. Enemy Rank								
	G	F	E	D	C	B	A	S
DAURAGON (OVERALLS)	G	F	E	D	C	B	A	S

SECRETS OF STORY MODE

ENDING EVENT SEQUENCE

As discussed in the Introduction and several other times throughout the book, there are multiple paths to take through the game. Events are shaped by the characters who experience them, and some scenes are only witnessed by using a particular character.

There are generally three endings to the game. The scenarios are essentially similar, but the perspective switches depending on which bouncer is chosen to fight

and defeat Dauragon. Each bouncer has his own individual Epilogue. Essentially, the player will want to clear the game three times to see all three Epilogues, using a different bouncer to defeat Dauragon each time.

Now come, Sion. I want you to show me

ever, the different Epilogues are just the tip of the iceberg. You can noticeably alter the dialogues
g the ending event sequence of the game by your choice of character in certain key
arios. Minor characters suddenly play more pivotal roles, and unique incidents occur onboard the
s. Character choice in the following three major sequences during the game affects the ending
t sequence:

The bouncer chosen to infiltrate the Mikado Building after the first battle with Dauragon.

The bouncer chosen to fight the Black Panther in the Galeos Hallway.

The bouncer chosen to fight Dauragon in the final battle.

only does the ending event sequence change depending on who is chosen in these particular events and battles, but hidden Epilogues occur
more hidden characters become available in Versus and Survival Modes.

cribed below are some particular events from the ending event sequence, how to make them occur, and any hidden characters that are
aled as a result. A complete flowchart follows to further demonstrate the path variations of the ending event sequence.

KALDEA DIES VIOLENTLY

If the player chooses Sion to infiltrate the Mikado Building, then Kaldea will
die a rather shocking death after the fight with the Black Panther in the
Galeos corridor.

I'll be all right...

KALDEA LIVES!

If the player chooses Volt or Kou to infiltrate the Mikado Building,
and then later chooses Sion to fight the Black Panther in the
Galeos corridor, Kaldea will live.

The separation sequence is starting!

KALDEA SHOWS THE WAY

If Kaldea lives after the Black Panther fight (following the formula described in "Kaldea Lives") and you
choose Sion to fight Dauragon, Kaldea will show the bouncers the escape route onboard the Galeos.

SION MEETS DOMINIQUE

Defeat Dauragon using Sion. After the credits roll, a brief scene
depicts the first encounter between Sion and Dominique.

Sion...

The Galeos is programmed to separate once
it gets near the satellite.

LEANN'S URGENT MESSAGE

If you use Kou to infiltrate the Mikado Building and fight Dauragon onboard the Galeos without
triggering the "Kaldea Shows the Way" sequence, then Leann will send the bouncers an urgent
message through the Galeos' communication system.

KOU FIGHTS LEANN

If you choose Kou to infiltrate the Mikado Building and defeat Dauragon onboard the Galeos, then Leann Caldwell will appear during Kou's Epilogue and challenge him to a fight. If you win the battle, then Leann is unlocked in Versus and Survival Modes. (Detailed strategy is described in the next section.)

MEMORIES OF MASTER WONG

You can unlock Master Wong in Versus and Survival Modes by following a unique path in the game. Choose Volt or Kou to infiltrate the Mikado Building and fight the Black Panther onboard the Galeos, and then use Sion to defeat Dauragon. During Sion's Epilogue, he will flash back to the teachings of his old master. Wong will then challenge Sion to a fight and, if you win, Master Wong is unlocked in Versus and Survival Modes. (Detailed strategy is described in the next section.)

DAURAGON'S FINAL FORM

You can unlock Dauragon's fourth and final form (Shirtless) when you finish your third Extra Game play through. During the third game, the final battle onboard the Galeos will consist of *three rounds* instead of the usual two. Dauragon's final form can be extremely difficult to defeat or quite easy; it depends upon the BP exchange strategy used by the player during all three games. (Details and combat strategy are contained in the next section.)

ENDING EVENT SEQUENCE

Since there are multiple paths to choose throughout the game, the ending varies depending on your character selection in certain situations. For a complete breakdown of how the ending unfolds for each character, please refer to the "Game Flowchart" on page 121.

EXTRA GAME POINTERS

So you've cleared your first game of The Bouncer. Either it was too easy or a nice challenge. Now what?

To keep playing the game and rank up your bouncers even higher, or to unlock even more hidden characters, use the Extra Game option on the Story Mode menu to load your Clear Game save.

The different path variations in the Ending Event Sequence as described previously make it impossible to unlock all 15 playable characters in Versus and Survival Modes in just one game. There is one hidden character that only becomes available after the player has cleared three games. There are also enough minor sequence variations to warrant even more replays of Story Mode.

In addition, after a first game, your characters can't possibly be at Superior Rank, nor can you purchase all their Extra Skills in one or even two games. If you thought the first game was too easy, let's see how well you do in your second or third game against more advanced opponents at higher Ranks!

KOU'S ALTERNATE GESTURES

Here's a little easter egg found in The Bouncer. When replaying the game, start a new game with the subtitles set in Japanese and play as Kou. During the scene on the elevator, where Kou's phone rings, he will do completely different gestures to match the Japanese subtitles!

URTHER RANKING UP

ing up your characters in The Bouncer is like a fine art. Do you try to rank up all
characters evenly in the same strides, or do you build one character up at a
? These are the kinds of issues discussed in this section.

ual Ranking

ing up all your characters evenly seems to have a few pitfalls. This equal ranking
nique is accomplished by mixing up your character choice for battles throughout
ur games. Let's say you play three games this way, and by the end of your third
e all your bouncers are at or near Rank C (estimated from our own playing).
e listed the Bouncer Rank and Game Rank tables from the Introduction so that
can illustrate a point. If you have three bouncers at Rank C, then you've exchanged
ast 22200 BP (7400 BP spent on three bouncers). If you look on the Game Rank
t, that amount exchanged still puts you squarely at an overall Rank of C. The
s enemies of the game will still be roughly at your fighting level. However, it should
oted that your game is treading on thin ice. You need just 26640 BP to achieve a
e Rank B status, taking all the Bosses up to that difficulty level. That's just 8880
consumed per bouncer! This means that if you continue to rank up your bouncers
his manner, the Game Rank could go up to B but your bouncers will all still be
k at Rank C! How are you ever going to go three rounds against the final Boss?

e Character at a Time

ther way to attempt to clear three games and rank up your bouncers is to fight an
re game with one character, and then the next game with a different character,
a third game with the remaining character. However, it should be noted that the
d character can be poorly matched in an overly difficult third game. It can be very
cult to acquire BP to exchange for status upgrades and Extra Skills, and several of
more challenging fights can be tough to win with this poorly matched character.
Game Rank has far exceeded the rank of this character in this scenario, and the
mies have the advantage. We don't recommend this route either.

ternate Method

other method to follow is to use one bouncer for every battle in every game. By the
inning of a third game, a character should likely be at S Rank. Yet since *only* this
racter has consumed BP, the overall Game Rank will remain at C! Not only is it
y to defeat Bosses and enemies with this character, but it is also possible to use
other characters for non-Boss fights in the third game to improve their stats as
l. Because the Game Rank is at C Rank, each successful battle will net around 300
nus Points. That's a great amount of extra points for a lower-status character to
end.

on't Exchange BP

re's something else to consider: If you want the game to remain easy, then don't
change BP! Actually, you can exchange a little, but you have to spend less than 800
per bouncer (the Game Rank increases to F Rank at 2400 BP). This method
bles you to improve some stats without increasing the difficulty of the game. You
uld be able to get through three games just by learning your characters' best
oves and practicing them well. This is an important option to consider when you
ntually have to go three rounds with someone like Dauragon. Just how tough do
u really want that fight to be?

RANKING CHART FOR BOUNCERS

Bouncer Rank	BP Consumption
G-F	1000
F-E	2500
E-D	4700
D-C	7400
C-B	11100
B-A	16100
A-S	23400

GAME RANK CHART

Game Rank	BP Consumption
G-F	2400
F-E	6000
E-D	11280
D-C	17760
C-B	26640
B-A	38640
A-S	56160

BONUS BP CHART

Game Rank	Bonus BP
G	100
F	150
E	200
D	250
C	300
B	350
A	400
S	500

SECRET BOSS FIGHTS

The following section lists some of the secret Boss fights found in The Bouncer.

BATTLE 28
Dauragon IV

BOSS

SHIRTLESS DAURAGON'S STATUS CHART

Status	Rank							
	G	F	E	D	C	B	A	S
Life	150	165	180	195	210	225	240	255
Power	100	115	131	147	162	178	194	210
Defense	85	97	109	121	133	145	157	170
BP	350	466	583	700	816	933	1050	1400

BOSS

SHIRTLESS DAURAGON'S EXTRA SKILLS

Skill Name	Rank							
	G	F	E	D	C	B	A	S
Sonic Elbow	*	*	*	*	*	*	*	*
Dragon Spiral	*	*	*	*	*	*	*	*
Flying Dragon Kick	-	-	*	*	*	*	*	*
Rushing Beat	-	-	-	-	*	*	*	*

The Dragon Lord

To fight Dauragon's final form, you must clear the game twice. At the end of the third game, the final battle is extended for a third round. Needless to say, Dauragon is faster and stronger than ever in his hidden final form. The player must fight three rounds against Dauragon, without a chance to save the game. In addition, Life and Defense meters do *not* refill between fights. How does anyone survive this battle for three rounds?

The pleasure of fighting for the sake of fighting!

The player can make this battle harder or easier. It all depends upon how the player exchanges BP throughout the first three games. Refer to the "Extra Game Pointers" section to learn how exchanging BP can make Dauragon extremely tough or easy.

way to make this three-battle war against Dauragon easier is to use only one character for three
es. That character should be at S Rank by the beginning of a third game, and should have all of his
us upgrades and Extra Skills. *Do not use the other two bouncers.* If you use this tactic, the
e Rank will still be at C because of the lack of BP spent overall. Dauragon will be at C Rank in
ree forms, and your S Rank character has a much better chance of surviving, retaining some
nsive capability.

her way to fight this battle is to avoid spending any BP at all. By doing this, the game will never
any more difficult than it is initially. Even Dauragon will be Rank G throughout, and he'll have fewer
s up his sleeve. Just get really good at using the moves inherent to your characters, and you'll
a blast. For more specific details, please refer to a particular character's section of the Story
e chapter.

BATTLE 29
Master Wong

BOSS

WONG'S STATUS CHART

Status	Rank							
	G	F	E	D	C	B	A	S
Life	100	111	122	134	145	157	168	180
Power	110	126	142	159	175	192	208	225
Defense	100	111	122	134	145	157	168	180
BP	120	160	200	240	280	320	360	480

BOSS

WONG'S EXTRA SKILLS

Skill Name	Rank							
	G	F	E	D	C	B	A	S
Step-In Elbow	-	-	-	✳	✳	✳	✳	✳
Vertical Smasher	✳	✳	✳	✳	✳	✳	✳	✳
Launcher	✳	✳	✳	✳	✳	✳	✳	✳
Cross Break	-	✳	✳	✳	✳	✳	✳	✳
Silent Exploder	-	-	-	-	-	✳	✳	✳
Wyvern's Charge	-	-	-	✳	✳	✳	✳	✳

Honorable Master

You can unlock Master Wong in Versus and Survival Modes by following a certain path in Story Mode.
To do so, do the following:

◎ Choose Volt or Kou to infiltrate the Mikado Building and to fight the Black Panther onboard the
Galeos, and then use Sion to defeat Dauragon.

During the Epilogue, Sion will flash back to his last encounter with his former teacher. If you win Master Wong's challenge, then Wong will be unlocked in Versus and Survival Modes. If you use Sion inside the Mikado Building, the Wong flashback will not occur.

Master Wong fights with his own versions of many of Sion's moves as well as Dauragon's. It is strongly recommended that you attempt this fight with a low Game Rank, so that Sion is not terribly outmatched. If possible, level up Sion to S Rank and keep your Game Rank at C or B.

Master Wong will keep his Guard firmly raised until he sees an opening. You should do the same. Avo using moves that involve high jumps or slow spins. Attempt combos such as the Combo Side Kick (h,h,h) or the Triple Kick (m,M,m). The Double Uppercut (M,m) is also effective. Also, try a Double Uppercut followed by a Torpedo Kick (ES + m).

Even if Wong blocks an entire combination attack, it will lower his Defense status. Although Wong guards a lot, avoid trying the Buster Throw. The Torpedo Kick or Floating Mine are much better Extra Skills to use.

If you knock down Wong, run around behind him as he gets up and attack him from behind. Show no mercy. In a one-on-one fight, you can't let your opponent get back up and resume his battle stance!

Losing to Wong doesn't mean that you get sent back to the Title screen; the dialogue afterward will merely be different. Yo must defeat Wong to unlock him, so you may want to save you game so you can try this fight again some other time.

BATTLE 30
Leann

LEANN'S STATUS CHART

Status	Rank							
	G	F	E	D	C	B	A	S
Life	105	118	132	145	159	172	186	200
Power	95	107	120	133	146	159	172	185
Defense	110	123	137	150	164	177	191	205
BP	120	160	200	240	280	320	360	480

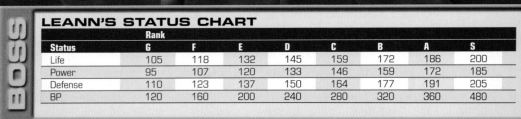

LEANN'S EXTRA SKILLS

Skill Name	Rank							
	G	F	E	D	C	B	A	S
Shuriken Kick	*	*	*	*	*	*	*	*
Rising Spinner	-	-	-	*	*	*	*	*
Shoulder Slam	-	*	*	*	*	*	*	*
Somersault Edge	-	-	-	-	-	*	*	*

I want you to go to the central plaza.

Dangers of the Superspy Business
If you use Kou to infiltrate the Mikado Building and then use him to defeat Dauragon, a special battle will occur during the Epilogue where Leann Caldwell challenges Kou to a fight. If you win, then Leann unlocked in Versus and Survival Modes.

Leann is a slender woman, but don't underestimate her strength. Exchanging jabs with her when she is C or B Rank is pretty crazy. Try to unlock Leann with a low Game Rank. If Kou is leveled up to S while the Game Rank remains C or B, then you gain a tremendous advantage.

hen Leann charges in, move Kou off the stairs and engage her in the flatter area. You should avoid fighting on steps or narrow, raised areas.
ann keeps her Guard up most of the time and so should you. She will attempt multiple attacks when you guard, specifically to weaken it.

ot of her moves involve jumping or spinning. You can counter these moves while she's attacking by quickly performing a simple Forward Kick (m)
Right Jab (h). This should knock her down, so follow it up with a Rolling Stomp (j). Or, Kou can avoid her attacks entirely by using the Slider
rection + l), and this may even knock her down in the process.

Against Leann, avoid using the Jump moves (except the Rolling Stomp in the situation mentioned above), Roundhouse Kicks, the Spinning Heel Drop, and the Heel Snap. That said, come to this fight with a few Extra Skills. Some of the best are the Circular Uppercut, the Double Spin Kick, and the Tiger Spin Kick.

Getting defeated by Leann doesn't send you back to the Title screen, but it does affect the subsequent dialogue. Frankly, the dialogue where Kou loses has a few surprises. The only way to unlock Leann in Versus and Survival Modes is to win this battle.

You're relieved of your assignment, of course.

LOADING SCREEN TRANSCRIPTS

Sometimes while the game is loading the next cinematic event in The Bouncer, a loading screen appears and displays the past of the character you have previously chosen. Since the game loads fairly quickly, it's sometimes difficult to read all of the text on-screen. Therefore, we've included all of the load screen text in this section so that you can learn even more about your favorite bouncers!

SION'S LOADING SCREENS

13 YEARS AGO

Wong: "Why do you follow me?"
Sion: "Will I ever be... as strong as you?"
Wong: "That is up to you."
Sion: "Hey, will you teach me?"
Wong: "It is my policy not to take any disciples. It is late... Go home."
Sion: "I... don't have a home..."

11 YEARS AGO

Sion: <huff> <huff>
Wong: "Giving up already?"
Sion: "N-No! I'm just hungry! Can't fight on an empty stomach!"
Wong: "Hmph... you are persistent... I'll give you that."
Sion: "Wh-What do I do... next?"
Wong: "Jump off of this cliff."
Sion: "A-All right..."
Wong: "Whoa whoa... I'm kidding! Come... It is time for dinner."

9 YEARS AGO

Girl: "What're you doing?"
Sion: "Can't you tell? I'm training!"
Girl: "Looks like a lot of fun."
Sion: "No one's stopping you from doing it."
Girl: "I get sick real easy, so..."
Sion: "... What's your name?"
Girl: "Kaldea."

YEARS AGO

n: "I finally made my master use one of his hands!"

dea: "Wow! You finally did it!"

n: "Yeah, but that geezer said it'd take me a lifetime to make him use both of his hands."

dea: "You two really do get along, don't you?"

n: "Kaldea, your parents are always kind and caring to you, too."

dea: "I've never been scolded my whole life. I don't know if you call that caring…"

YEARS AGO

dea: "What is it?"

n: "Master Wong… hasn't come home…"

dea: "What… ?"

n: "He said something weird a while ago… but I didn't expect him to disappear so suddenly…"

dea: "Have you notified the police? He could have been involved in some accident…"

n: "No accident could kill him! Even if someone tried to murder him… that old man wouldn't die…!"

YEARS AGO

n: "Here, congratulations."

dea: "Are you sure?"

n: "Of course! You got that job at Mikado, right?"

dea: "But… Can you afford this… ?"

n: "Don't worry."

dea: "Thank you. I'll treasure it."

n: "OK, but don't go locking it away in some box. It's a pendant. You're supposed to wear it."

YEARS AGO

n: "What do you mean an accident!?"

dea's Father: "There was an… accident at Mikado and…"

n: "And… what hospital is she in… ?"

dea's Mother: <sob> <sob>

dea's Father: "She… didn't make it…"

n: "Huh… ?"

dea's Father: "It was a… massive explosion…"

n: "You're lying…"

dea's Father: "S-Sion!"

n: "THAT'S A LIE!"

YEARS AGO

n: (Kaldea…)

n: "Hey! Watch it!"

n: (…)

n: "Who the hell do you think you are, running into me like that without an apology!? What's with the pathetic look on your face? What, did your girlfriend dump you?"

n: "Errr… raaaaaaaah!!"

1 YEAR AGO

Sion: "…"

Man: "Hey… Noticed you were looking at me. You got a problem with me or something?"

Sion: "C'mon…"

Man: "What!?"

Sion: "Why don't you go ahead and kill me…"

Man: "What are you on!?"

Sion: "That is… if you think you got what it takes…"

Man: "You're asking for it, you little… !!!"

1 YEAR AGO

Sion: "Someone! Anyone! Come and kill me!"

Sion: "Anyone!? You can use a gun if you have to!"

Young Man: "Uh… umm…"

Sion: "You're going to be the one to kill me?"

Young Man: "I think I know a man… who could get the job done…"

Sion: "Who is he?"

Young Man: "A man who works at a bar called Fate!"

1 YEAR AGO

Customer: "Ah-aaaaahhhhh!"

Boss: "Hey, hey, you're scaring my customers. Why don't you take it someplace else?"

Man: "I think that's my job, Boss."

Sion: "Those piercings make you look like a demon straight outta hell. You think you got what it takes to get me there?"

1 YEAR AGO

Sion: "I'm… not dead… yet…"

Volt: "Not bad… for a little kid…"

Boss: "What do you think about working for me, boy?"

Sion: "What… ?"

Boss: "He works for me as a bouncer. It's your choice. No one's going to stop you from leaving if you want to…"

Sion: "All right, I'll do it… But only until I can beat him… !"

VOLT'S LOADING SCREENS

5 YEARS AGO

Boy A: "Dammit! We've been had!"
Boy B: "I told you! We shouldn't have pushed it while he was away…"
Boy A: "D-Damn… !"
A Voice: "You're right about that."
Boy B: "V-Volt!"

5 YEARS AGO

Man: "Guh… hua!"
Volt: "Giving up already?"
Mob Boss: "Impressive! Most impressive!"
Volt: "!"
Mob Boss: "You just tore through one of my best men like a dog on a rag doll. How 'bout you pull a job for me?"
Volt: "Why should I… ?"
Mob Boss: "I need someone erased… In exchange for your services, I'll keep my hands off your turf…"
Volt: "…"

5 YEARS AGO

Agent: "It's impossible… We can't stop him!?"
A Voice: "Cease your attacks. He's far more than any of us can handle."
Agent: "M-Master Mikado!"
Mikado: "It appears he has some business to settle with me."
Agent: "Stay in the car, sir! It's far too dangerous out here!"
Mikado: "It won't have made a difference whether I'm in the car or not."
Volt: "You… aren't afraid?"

5 YEARS AGO

Woman: "So… you're the new rookie?"
Volt: "You're an agent as well?"
Woman: "The name's Aena Paula. Codename: Echidna."
Volt: "Who would've thought they'd make a woman an agent."
Echidna: "Hey, don't underestimate me. You know as well as I do that you've gotta be damn good to work as a security agent here."

5 YEARS AGO

Mikado: "Have you ever thought about working for me?"
Volt: "I've come here to kill you."
Mikado: "And thanks to that, I was able to meet you. Don't worry. I'll have a word with that 'organization.'"
Volt: "Who are you… ?"

4 YEARS AGO

Volt: "Echidna, get Master Mikado to safety!"
Echidna: "What about you, Volt!?"
Volt: "I can handle this myself just fine."
Echidna: "Are you crazy!? You're gonna get slaughtered!"
Mikado: "Let's trust Volt."
Volt: "Get going, Echidna!"
Echidna: "<tch>… !"

3 YEARS AGO

Echidna: "I challenge you…"
Volt: "What… ?"
Echidna: "I've always wanted to go up against you."
Volt: "Unfortunately, I'm on duty protecting Master Mikado. And it's against my principles to raise my hand against a woman."
Echidna: "<tch>… !"
A Voice: "I see that man is an eyesore to you…"
Echidna: "Huh… ?"

3 YEARS AGO

Volt: (Master Mikado… Forgive me… ! I should not have taken my eyes off you…)
Echidna: "You seem to be in agony, Volt."
Volt: "Echidna! You were with Master Mikado! How could you let him… !"
Echidna: "It couldn't be helped. I'm much weaker than you. I couldn't protect him…"
Volt: "Why you… !"

3 YEARS AGO

Volt: "What're you trying to say, Echidna?"
Echidna: "Now, I'll be the one to move ahead… Once I deal with you the one who conspired in the death of Master Mikado!"
Volt: "What!?"
Echidna: "FIRE!"
Volt: "Echidnaaaaaa!"

3 YEARS AGO

Man: "Looks like you've come to."
Volt: "Where am I… ?"
Man: "I found you out on the shore."
Volt: "Why am I here… ?"
Man: "I assumed you wouldn't want the cops or docs involved."
Volt: "…"
Man: "I did a lot of crazy things when I was your age, too."

3 YEARS AGO

Man: "You got a place to go?"
Volt: "I don't want to trouble you anymore than I have to."
Man: "You interested in a job at my bar? It sure would help if I had a bouncer like you."
Volt: "A bouncer, eh… ?"

2 YEARS AGO

Volt: "Well, if it's okay with you… I wouldn't mind working as a bouncer
Boss: "But the gunshot wound on your forehead's gonna attract som unwanted attention. How 'bout we cover it up with some bod piercings? But the only thing that would work on that spot would be some horns."
Volt: "Horns, eh… ? That might actually be appropriate."

KOU'S LOADING SCREENS

7 YEARS AGO

cher: "Your boy is a genius. Not only scholastically: he is also musically and artistically very talented."

ther: "Indeed. I want him to bring honor to the Hurst family name."

u: "I'd like to learn martial arts, too."

ther: "Absolutely not! What if something happened to you!"

3 YEARS AGO

u: "Mother, I have a favor to ask you... I really want to learn Tae Kwon Do."

ther: "No son of mine will learn martial arts! How many times must I tell you!?"

u: "Then I will leave this house! I believe in order to be a proper heir to the Hurst family, one must be strong, as well!"

ther: "... !"

1 YEARS AGO

and Master: "It is amazing. I never expected someone your age to be able to go hand-to-hand with me. If I had my way, I would have you inherit this dojo."

u: "Really!?"

and Master: "But that is not possible. You are the heir of the Hurst family."

u: "..."

YEARS AGO

other: "You earned a doctorate at such a young age. I'm so proud of u. You are indeed a Hurst..."

u: "I'm sorry, but... as of today, I renounce that name. I appreciate my birth into the Hurst family, and I do appreciate the education you have provided me. However, I've learned something more important from Tae Kwon Do."

other: "Wh-What are you saying!?"

u: "From now on, I will live on with my master's name: Leifoh."

4 YEARS AGO

nior Officer: "So you are the elite they've been harping about."

u: "I'm not elite. I'm just here to do a job that's worth risking my life over."

nior Officer: "Heh... You passed. According to our reports, it appears you are from the Hurst family. Depending on your reaction, I was going to disqualify you."

3 YEARS AGO

nior Officer: "Allow me to introduce your partner for the next mission."

u: "A... A woman?"

oman: "I've got a name; it's Leann Caldwell."

nior Officer: "Her survival abilities may be higher than yours."

u: "..."

ann: "Is there something on my face?"

3 YEARS AGO

ann: "I screwed up. I didn't expect them to have so many on reserve..."

u: "You can make it out of here alone, right?"

ann: "Alone... ? What're you going to do?"

u: "I'll draw their attention."

ann: "That's suicide!"

u: "Just trust me. And if we make it out of here alive, you owe me a drink."

ann: "... I'll think about it."

2 YEARS AGO

Kou: "Hey! Heard you were promoted! Congratulations!"

Leann: "I told high-command that it was all because of you..."

Kou: "No, it was because of your talent. Oh yeah, by the way, you still remember that promise we made?"

Leann: "Huh?"

Kou: "You owe me a drink."

1 YEAR AGO

Leann: "Did you call for me, sir?"

Senior Officer: "Here... I knew Mikado's solar energy plan sounded fishy."

Leann: "And there's also information about surgical enhancements in here..."

Senior Officer: "This mission's going to be our toughest yet..."

Leann: "Rest assured, I'm confident he will be able to pull it off."

6 MONTHS AGO

Kou: "A full-body tattoo? What the hell kind of mission is this? I'm just supposed to watch over the girl, right?"

Leann: "That's not all. It's also your job to prevent her from falling into the hands of the Mikado Group."

Kou: "You mean that mega-corporation!?"

Leann: "If all else fails, your job is to eliminate her..."

6 MONTHS AGO

Boss: "You're an unfamiliar face."

Kou: "Yeah, just moved into town... hoping to find a job."

Boss: "This place used to be pretty busy, thanks to Mikado, but lately they haven't been outsourcing much of their work."

Kou: "<sigh>... We've hit some bad times. Drinking seems to help the time pass, though..."

3 MONTHS AGO

Man: "Agh... !"

Boss: "Not bad. Not bad at all for someone like you."

Dominique: "Boss, why don't you hire Kou as a bouncer, too?"

Boss: "Hey, hey, you know how expensive it is for me just to keep two bouncers."

Dominique: "I'll help clean the bar!"

Boss: "Ahhh, fine, fine... It's only because you insist on it, Dominique..."

Kou: "I admire your good taste, princess!"

GAME FLOWCHART

BATTLE 1
vs. MSF
Location: "FATE" Bar

BATTLE 2
vs. MSF
Location: Central Square

BATTLE 3
vs. Security Guards
Location: Central Station

BATTLE 4
vs. Security Guards
Location: Central Station (timed)

BATTLE 5
vs. Security Guards
Location: MSD Cargo Train

BATTLE 6
vs. Echidna & Security Guards
Location: MSD Cargo Train

BATTLE 7a
vs. Security Chiefs & Security Guards
Location: Emergency Passageway (Normal Scenario)
*Requirement: Finding Card Key

BATTLE 7b
vs. Security Chief, Commander & Security Guards
Location: Emergency Passageway (Closing Shutters Scenario)
*Requirement: Cannot Find Card Key

BATTLE 8
vs. Carrier Soldiers
Location: Air Carrier

BATTLE 9
vs. MSF & Watchdogs
Location: Mikado Building/
Hanging Garden

BATTLE 10
vs. Mugetsu & MSF
Location: Mikado Building/
Hanging Garden

BATTLE 11
vs. Dauragon & Black Panther
Location: Crystal Dome

To Character Selection (page 119)

CHARACTER SELECTION

VOLT

SION

KOU

BATTLE 12
vs. Security Guards
Location: Mikado Building
(65F Hall)

BATTLE SURPRISE
vs. Commander & P-101
Location: Mikado Building
(65F Conference Room)

BATTLE SURPRISE
vs. MSF
Location: Mikado Building
(65F Elevators)

BATTLE 13
vs. P-101s & Security Guards
Location: Mikado Building
(66F Meeting Room)

BATTLE 16
vs. MSF
Location: Mikado Building
(Enhancement Surgery Area)

BATTLE 18
vs. MSF
Location: MFB Room

BATTLE 14
vs. MSF Elite & MSF
Location: Mikado Building
(Data Room)

BATTLE 17
vs. MSF Elite, P-101s & MSF
Location: Mikado Building
(Bio-Plant/Robot Factory)

BATTLE 15
vs. Black Panther
Location: Executive Office
Hallway

BATTLE MINI GAME
Kou Infiltration Mini-Game
Location: Mikado Building

BOUNCERS UNITE

To Battle 19 (page 120)

GAME FLOWCHART

BATTLE 19

vs. Mugetsu, MSF Elite, & MSF
Location: Executive Office

BATTLE 20

vs. Multiple Enemies
Location: Rocket Tower (6F to 2F)

BATTLE 21

vs. PD-4
Location: Rocket Tower

Three on one...
Those are acceptable odds...

BATTLE 22

vs. LD-X1 & LD-15
Location: Rocket Tower (Basement)

BATTLE 23

vs. Echidna & LD-X1s
Location: Rocket Tower (Basement)

Once I defeat all of YOU!

BATTLE 24

vs. Mugetsu
Location: Air-Carrier

BATTLE 25

vs. Black Panther
Location: Galeos Passageway

CHARACTER SELECTION

Who Navigates the Way?
See additional flowcharts to determine each character's ending.

BATTLE 26

vs. Dauragon (Normal)
Location: Galeos Control Room

BATTLE 27

vs. Dauragon (Overalls)
Location: Galeos Control Room

ADDITIONAL

BATTLE 28

vs. Dauragon (Shirtless)
Location: Galeos Control Room
Requirement: Only occurs during third play-through

le players can also fight up to three CPU-controlled opponents. Set each player to CPU or None, depending on how many characters would like to fight. The more opponents you take on, the tougher and more intense the match is. There are also options available to the length of the match and how many victorious rounds are required to win the game. At the end of each battle, the character has a ety of taunts, depending on how well you fight.

Team Battle

RULES: In Team Battle, two teams of three characters go head-to-head to determine the winner. Each player selects which character they are going to control (the Leader), plus two CPU-controlled allies to fight as a team of three. Or, one player and two CPU teammates can battle it out against an all-CPU team. The battle ends when the leader is defeated. There are also options you can use to vary the length of the rounds and the number of rounds required for a player to win the game. The best strategy to employ is to go after the other leader, hoping that your CPU teammates can chip in and help.

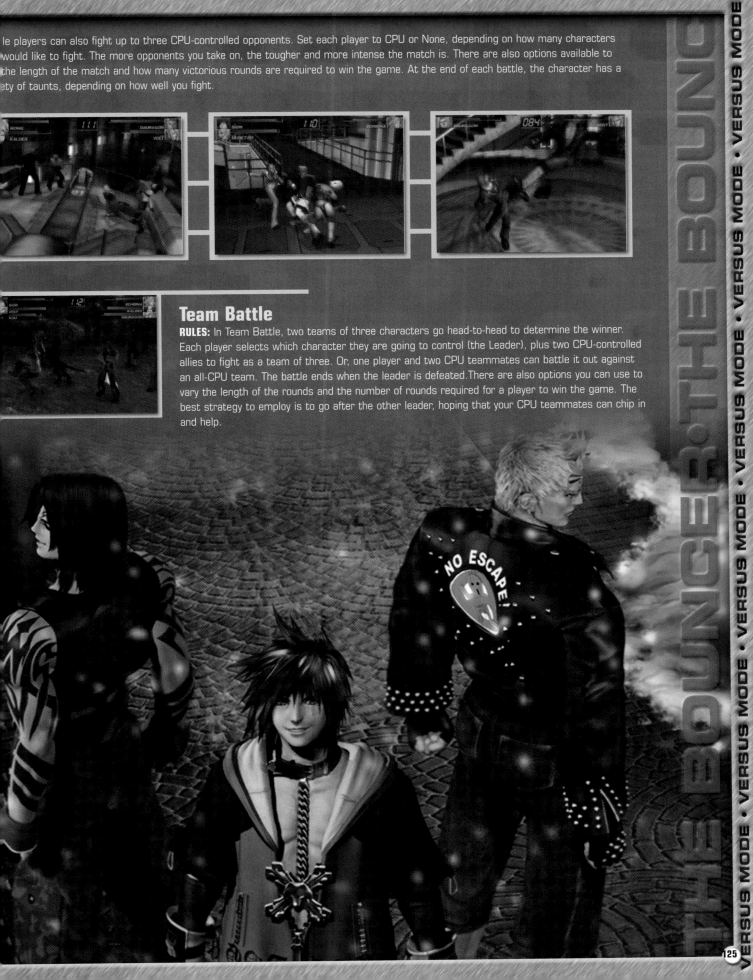

SURVIVAL MODE

In Survival Mode, a player can use characters unlocked in Story Mode to attempt to defeat as many enemies as possible before the character's Life meter is reduced to zero. There are 10 Stages and the player's Life meter does NOT refill between each stage. All opponents must be KO'd in each stage to progress to the next stage.

Players can select from up to 15 characters, which are unlocked by playing Story Mode. You can press the R2, L1, and L2 buttons on the controller before selecting characters to choose alternate costumes (see the Unlockable Characters section for more details). Hidden character ranking is determined by the Rank at which the character was fought in Story Mode, which is based on overall Game Rank.

A total of 50 opponents appear throughout the various stages in Survival Mode. Whether or not you defeat all 50, the player is given an alphanumerical ranking based on fighting ability. The total number of KO's and your time determine the player's Ranking in Survival Mode.

SURVIVAL STAGES

This section contains a list of tables showing the Rank of the enemies in each stage compared to the overall Game Rank of whatever saved game you are using.

As you can tell by comparing these charts, Survival Mode becomes progressively more difficult as you clear more stages. You have a better chance of getting all the way through and defeating all 50 enemies with a character of Rank S. That is, unless you are some kind of fighting god!

SURVIVAL STAGE 01

Enemy	Game Rank vs. Enemy Rank							
	G	F	E	D	C	B	A	S
MSF	G	G	G	G	G	G	G	G
MSF	F	F	F	F	F	F	F	F
SECURITY GUARD	G	G	G	G	G	G	G	G
SECURITY GUARD	F	F	F	F	F	F	F	F

SURVIVAL STAGE 02

Enemy	Game Rank vs. Enemy Rank							
	G	F	E	D	C	B	A	S
SECURITY CHIEF	G	G	G	G	G	G	G	G
SECURITY CHIEF	F	F	F	F	F	F	F	F
SECURITY CHIEF	E	E	E	E	E	E	E	E
COMMANDER	G	G	G	G	G	G	G	G
COMMANDER	F	F	F	F	F	F	F	F

SURVIVAL STAGE 03

Enemy	Game Rank vs. Enemy Rank							
	G	F	E	D	C	B	A	S
P-101	F	F	F	F	F	F	F	F
P-101	E	E	E	E	E	E	E	E
P-101	D	D	D	D	D	D	D	D
CARRIER SOLDIER	F	F	F	F	F	F	F	F
CARRIER SOLDIER	E	E	E	E	E	E	E	E
CARRIER SOLIDER	D	D	D	D	D	D	D	D

SURVIVAL STAGE 04

Enemy	Game Rank vs. Enemy Rank							
	G	F	E	D	C	B	A	S
WATCHDOG	E	E	E	E	E	E	E	E
WATCHDOG	D	D	D	D	D	D	D	D
WATCHDOG	C	C	C	C	C	C	C	C
MC-07	F	F	F	F	F	F	F	F
MC-07	E	E	E	E	E	E	E	E

SURVIVAL STAGE 05

Enemy	Game Rank vs. Enemy Rank							
	G	F	E	D	C	B	A	S
LD-X1	D	D	D	D	D	D	D	D
LD-15	C	C	C	C	C	C	C	C
MSF ELITE	C	C	C	C	C	C	C	C
MSF	D	D	D	D	D	D	D	D
MSF	C	C	C	C	C	C	C	C

SURVIVAL STAGE 06

Enemy	Game Rank vs. Enemy Rank							
	G	F	E	D	C	B	A	S
P-101	A	A	A	A	A	A	A	A
P-101	B	B	B	B	B	B	B	B
MC-07	A	A	A	A	A	A	A	A
MC-07	B	B	B	B	B	B	B	B
MC-07	C	C	C	C	C	C	C	C
MC-07	D	D	D	D	D	D	D	D

SURVIVAL STAGE 07

Enemy	Game Rank vs. Enemy Rank							
	G	F	E	D	C	B	A	S
SECURITY GUARD	S	S	S	S	S	S	S	S
SECURITY CHIEF	S	S	S	S	S	S	S	S
COMMANDER	S	S	S	S	S	S	S	S
CARRIER SOLIDER	S	S	S	S	S	S	S	S
WATCHDOG	A	A	A	A	A	A	A	A
WATCHDOG	B	B	B	B	B	B	B	B
WATCHDOG	C	C	C	C	C	C	C	C

SURVIVAL STAGE 08

Enemy	Game Rank vs. Enemy Rank							
	G	F	E	D	C	B	A	S
P-101	S	S	S	S	S	S	S	S
MC-07	S	S	S	S	S	S	S	S
LD-15	S	S	S	S	S	S	S	S
LD-X1	S	S	S	S	S	S	S	S

SURVIVAL STAGE 09

Enemy	Game Rank vs. Enemy Rank							
	G	F	E	D	C	B	A	S
WATCHDOG	S	S	S	S	S	S	S	S
WATCHDOG	A	A	A	A	A	A	A	A
MSF ELITE	S	S	S	S	S	S	S	S
MSF ELITE	A	A	A	A	A	A	A	A
MSF	S	S	S	S	S	S	S	S
MSF	A	A	A	A	A	A	A	A
MSF	A	A	A	A	A	A	A	A

SURVIVAL STAGE 10

Enemy	Game Rank vs. Enemy Rank							
	G	F	E	D	C	B	A	S
SION (BLACK)	S	S	S	S	S	S	S	S

SURVIVAL MODE: FIGHTING STRATEGIES

The following section details some helpful fighting tips to employ when playing through the Survival Mode of The Bouncer.

SION BARZAHD

Sion lacks effective moves for use in open areas, which makes it difficult for him to battle multiple enemies. This being the case, avoid getting surrounded, and instead create one-on-one fighting situations. When facing a lone enemy, use the "Hit-and-Retreat" method to gradually reduce the enemy's HP.

You can also lead an enemy in front of you, and use the Corkscrew Punch (h,H) or the Torpedo Kick (ES + m) to knock down multiple enemies at once.

Recommended Moves

Sion's Cyclone Kick (J) can damage multiple enemies in a wide area. You can use it effectively in a one-on-one situation or when surrounded by enemies. Try using the Jab (h) and Combo Side Kick (h,h,h) together to knock down an enemy and then move on to the next one. Another powerful combo for a one-on-one situation is a mid-air combo starting with an Uppercut (M).

VOLT KRUEGER

Volt's moves are rather slow, which makes Survival Mode difficult. However, you can optimize his intense attack power by guarding effectively and damaging an enemy at a slow rate. Also, rely on Volt's Extra Skill throw moves! Throw moves inflict high damage, plus you still retain distance between you and your enemy.

On the downside, throw moves are ineffective against robots. Instead, you must rely on attacks other than throws.

Recommended Moves

The Hammer Typhoon (ES + m) is a good non-throw move. It covers a wide area, so use it when surrounded by enemies. You can also use it to lure enemies in front of you to knock them all down at once.

Volt's Giant Swing (ES + l + j) is a great throw move. When using it, first use the Shoulder Uppercut (ES + h) and then run toward the fallen enemy right into a Giant Swing!

KOU LEIFOH

Make use of Kou's combination moves. Against Security Guards, use a Circular Uppercut (ES + m) followed by a Lightnin Smash (ES + l + j). Other effective moves for use in open areas include the Double Spin Kick (ES + j) or the Tiger Frenzy (ES + h + j). When fighting robots, use the Raging Tiger (ES + h + m). Against the small P-101 robots, the Heel Smash (ES + l) and the Circular Uppercut are very effective.

Recommended Moves

Kou's Extra Skill kicks are by far the best! The Heel Smash is a good choice for Low attacks or when executing a Running attack. To knock down enemies, use the Double Spin Kick (ES + j) or the Tiger Spin Kick (ES + l + m). In one-on-one fights use the Circular Uppercut as a combo to juggle an enemy.

KALDEA

It's best to fight as the Black Panther (which enables you to stay low (ES + l to transform)), because the Guards and MS rely on High attacks. The Black Panther is also effective against smaller enemies like Watchdogs and P-101s. Use the Ta Attack (L) and the Low Scratch (l), which may prove more effective because of its speed.

Recommended Moves

As the Black Panther, use the Spinning Rush Extra Skill (ES + h) because of its decent range. Although you are susceptib to an enemy attack while executing the Spinning Rush, you can attack in sequence, which makes it effective against large robots in particular.

DAURAGON

Dauragon's offense is his best defense. Strike with his powerful moves and take out the enemy quickly. However, this strategy becomes less effective in later stages because the enemies are more powerful.

Against smaller enemies (like Watchdogs and P-101s), Dauragon may struggle. Against a P-101, rely on the Spinning Fan (j). Against the Watchdogs, use sweep attacks.

Recommended Moves

The Spinning Fan and the Double Sweep (l,L), moves possessed by all four of his versions, are extremely effective attacks. Although Dauragon's attacks vary for each of his four versions, the following notes are standard for all four types.

- ◎ The speed of the attack.
- ◎ The power of the attack.
- ◎ Dauragon's chances of being counterattacked after initiating the attack. (The attack's recovery time.)

ONE-ARMED DAURAGON

Dauragon struggles in close combat situations, so attack from a distance using the Elbow Spear (ES + h + m). It should be noted that this move is difficult to block. The Triple Rave Kick (ES + h [x3]) is another quick attack with good range.

NORMAL DAURAGON

When fighting in close quarters, use the Dragon Claw (ES + h). This move is fast and powerful and can inflict damage against smaller enemies. The Crescent Moon Slash (ES + j), although it has less range, can dish out two hits if you're close to the enemy.

OVERALLS DAURAGON

When attacking from a distance, use the Launcher (ES + j). When using this move, Dauragon lowers his body, which enables him to dodge High attacks. The Sonic Elbow (ES + m) is effective when battling in close range. When fighting from a distance, use the Lunging Strike (Direction + m) to close in and follow up with the Sonic Elbow. You can replace the Sonic Elbow with the Launcher in this combo.

SHIRTLESS DAURAGON

Overalls Dauragon and Shirtless Dauragon are nearly identical fighters, and both possess the Sonic Elbow Extra Skill (ES + m). As Shirtless Dauragon, attack with close-combat fighting moves. His powerful Flying Dragon Kick (ES + j) has great range and causes big damage even when blocked. Use his Rushing Beat (ES + m + l) to fight robotic enemies.

DOMINIQUE

Dominique has low stamina, which makes clearing Survival Mode somewhat difficult. This being the case, you should strengthen her Guard. Fight in one-on-one battles, and avoid getting surrounded by multiple enemies. Attack with Dominique's Rising Spin Kick (H) and Ground Spin Kick (M,m) to dodge High attacks. Against Watchdogs, attack with the Spike Bomber (ES + j) or the Slide Kick (L).

Recommended Moves

The Destruction Uppercut (ES + h) is effective during close combat. This is one of her most powerful moves and it has a short recovery time, which may prevent some counterattacks.

The Spike Bomber is effective when fighting smaller enemies. The Dominique Bounce (Direction + m) is a good choice against charging enemies.

MUGETSU (WITH MASK)

Keep your distance from an enemy and then close with speedy attacks and combos. Mugetsu lacks a wide-range attack, so don't get surrounded. If it does happen, use Sweep (L) or Hi-Getsu (ES + j) to break free.

The Jab (h) to Heel Drop (h,h,h) combo deals damage to the small P-101. After knocking it against a wall and using this combo, you'll have no worries of a counterattack.

Recommended Moves

With the Hi-Getsu Rush (ES + j [x2]), Mugetsu charges in head first with both arms spread open. This move is quick and it has a wide attack range. You can use the Hi-Getsu Rush to knock out multiple enemies in close quarters, or to initiate a preemptive strike from a distance.

MUGETSU (WITHOUT MASK)

In Mugetsu's (no mask) case, the strategy of trying to push your enemies back with combo strikes is unfavorable, sin the recovery time after his attacks is quite long. This is especially apparent when fighting against robots and will ofte be countered by a damaging blow.

Use a "Hit-and-Retreat" tactic in which Mugetsu rushes in from a distance and causes damage with a lone attack. Against human enemies, avoid getting surrounded and rely on Middle attacks. The Ren-Getsu Extra Skill (ES + h + m a Guard-cancel attack, so use it only when you're surrounded.

Recommended Moves

The Crazy Drill (Direction + m) is possibly your best choice, due to its speed and striking distance. Use the Crazy Dri when battling multiple enemies. Keep in mind that you may get counterattacked because of this move's long recovery time.

ECHIDNA

Echidna's strategy revolves around long-range attacks. She doesn't possess the greatest attack power, so your fights may last a while. Occasionally, you may get countered between attacks. With this in mind, you should avoid using moves that will leave you unguarded and use many small attacks.

Recommended Moves

The Headspin (m,M) is one of Echidna's most cherished moves. This spin kick move stems from her lateral kick, Mei Lua Reversão (m). It has a wide attack range and a short recovery time.

The best thing about this move is that even if the first attack (Mei Lua Reversão) is blocked, the Headspin will conne on the enemy when their Guard is lowered.

LEANN

It's important to get Leann in and out of combat range. Since she lacks power, rely on her speed to find openings against a group of enemies. To counter her lack of power, execute multiple, smaller moves.

Use the Twin Blade (j) combos when battling robots, and attack Watchdogs with the Backside Low Kick (L). Against the P-101s, the Side Step Kick (M) works well.

Recommended Moves

Leann's Rising Spinner Extra Skill (ES + j) is an effective choice. Although it has short range, it hits a wide area so perform it when close to an enemy.

PD-4

Attacking from a distance is key when fighting as PD-4. The Straight Punch (m,m,m) attack is good against P-101s. When performing the Lightning Whip (ES + m), keep in mind that it shifts an enemy's position just slightly so make sure you're facing the enemy and adjust the distance before attacking again.

Recommended Moves

PD-4's most crucial attack is the Lightning Whip. You can actually dominate a fight with just this one move. Against t slow moving robotic enemies, the Lightning Viper (ES + h + m) is quite useful.

WONG

Let the enemies come toward you before attacking. Many of Wong's moves will knock an enemy into the air, so try to knock enemies into each other. Since Wong lacks strong combos, he falls prey to robots. You should rely on moves w short recovery times when fighting them.

Recommended Moves

The Vertical Smasher (ES + m), one of Wong's strongest attacks, covers a great distance and has a short recovery time. It launches an enemy into the air, so try to knock down other enemies in the area.

Use Wong's Step-In Elbow (ES + h) to close the distance with enemies. The Elbow Strike (M) and Forward Jump Kick (J) are very effective in close combat situations.

GENERAL TIPS

Guarding is crucial. Survival Mode has a total of 10 stages in which the player will *not* recover Life. To defeat all 50 enemies, you must keep damage at a minimum. Don't overlook enemy movements and make sure you guard when attacked. If you guard against an attack, it is much easier to catch the enemy off-guard right after the attack.

Remember enemy locations. Enemies appearing in a stage are placed in designated areas, so it's important to remember where they are located. This makes it much easier to develop an attack plan throughout the whole stage. Also, knowing enemy locations will enable the player to shave off time for the Rankings.

Lure enemies into battle. If you come into close contact with an enemy, that enemy will always move towards your fighter. Knowing this, you can lure enemies into an advantageous position or to an area where you can isolate the enemy. For example, you can lure several enemies into one area and knock them down at once, or lure enemies into a narrow corridor to create a one-on-one situation.

Vary your moves. If you constantly use Extra Skills in battle, the enemy will eventually catch you off-guard, thus making you vulnerable to unnecessary attacks. To avoid this, learn the in-and-outs of each character's moves (for example, recovery time and the number of times an attack will hit). Try using moves that inflict heavy damage on slow and bulky enemies, while relying on regular attacks with quick recovery time against enemies that constantly attack.

SURVIVAL MODE SECRETS

Black-hooded Sion. Defeat the black-hooded Sion in Survival Mode to unlock Sion's black-hooded costume. To access it in Versus and Survival Mode, press R1 + R2 + L1 + L2.

- **Kou's MSF disguise.** After infiltrating the Mikado Building with Kou, you receive Kou's MSF disguise. To access it in Versus and Survival Mode, press R1 + R2 + L1 + L2.

UNLOCKABLE CHARACTERS

There are a total of 15 characters who you can unlock and use to fight in Versus Mode and Survival Mode. To unlock these characters, you must meet certain conditions, which depend upon the player's progress in Story Mode.

An unlocked character's Rank, Status, and available Extra Skills are determined by the player's overall Game Rank. Just as characters become more difficult to fight as the player's Game Rank increases, they become stronger characters to use in Versus and Survival Mode if you can defeat them in Story Mode.

Each character has the following costumes:

⊚   Regular costume worn in Story Mode, available in two to four colors.

⊚   Select an alternate costume by holding the L1, L2, or R2 Buttons while selecting a character.

Character Rank is indicated in the selection screen of either Survival Mode or Versus Mode. The tables for each character in this section determine the level of their statuses and which Extra Skills they will possess as a result of their Rank. In the Available Extra Skills charts, a (-) indicates that the skill is not yet learned, while an (*) indicates the Ranks at which an Extra Skill is acquired.

ECHIDNA

Age: 25   Height: 5'5"   Fighting Style: Brazilian "Capoeira"

...executive member of the Mikado Group, Echidna is an unyielding and ...oud warrior. Power and status are her only desires, which makes her ...rive to move up in the organization. Echidna's loud wardrobe and ...ique hairstyle are her trademarks. She shared some connection with ...lt in the past...

ALTERNATE COSTUMES

Echidna Blue.
(R2 Button)

Echidna Black Tux.
(L1 Button)

Echidna White Tux.
(L2 Button)

UNLOCKING ECHIDNA

...unlock Echidna in Versus and Survival Modes, you must defeat her in ...attle 6 onboard the MSD Cargo Train. Her Rank improves each time ...u defeat her in Story Mode, based on your overall Game Rank.

ECHIDNA'S STATUS CHART

Status	Rank							
	G	F	E	D	C	B	A	S
Life	110	122	135	148	161	174	187	200
Power	80	93	107	120	134	147	161	175
Defense	90	106	122	139	155	172	188	205
BP	120	160	200	240	280	320	360	480

AVAILABLE EXTRA SKILLS

Skill Name	Rank							
	G	F	E	D	C	B	A	S
Missile Kick	*	*	*	*	*	*	*	*
Cyclone Drive	-	*	*	*	*	*	*	*
Dead-End Carnival	-	-	*	*	*	*	*	*
Double Slap	-	-	-	*	*	*	*	*
Ambush Strike	-	-	-	-	*	*	*	*

ECHIDNA'S MOVES LIST

Type	Name	Command	Base Damage
Jump	Armada Dupla	j	19
Jump	Parafuso	J	20
High	Right Punch	h	9
High	One-Two Punch	h,h	10
High	Backhand	h,h,h	12
High	Handstand Kick	h,h,h,h	25
High	Armada	H	18
High	Au Batido	h,H	21
Middle	Mei Lua Reversao	m	10
Middle	Au de Costa	M	13
Middle	Headspin	m,M	15
Middle	Benção	Direction + m	24
Low	Leg Sweep	l	8
Low	Heel Stomp	L	8
	2nd hit	L (x2)	8
Low	Helicopter Spin	l,L	12
Low	Rasteira	l,L,l	12
Low	Double Rasteira	l,L,l,l	20

Type	Name	Command	Base Damage
ES1	Missile Kick	ES + j	27
ES2	Cyclone Drive*	ES + l	14
	2nd hit	ES + l (x2)	14
	3rd hit	ES + l (x3)	13-23
ES3	Dead-End Carnival**	ES + h	14
	2nd hit	ES + h (x2)	14
	3rd hit	ES + h (x3)	15
	4th hit	ES + h (x4)	26
ES4	Double Slap	ES + m	25
	2nd hit	ES + m (x2)	35
ES5	Ambush Strike	ES + h + m, h, (m)	32

*You can repeat this move by continuously pressing the Low attack button.
**You can repeat this move by continuously pressing the High attack button.

MUGETSU

Age: 30?   Height: 5'11"   Fighting Style: Profane/Insane Arts

...he leader of the Mikado Special Forces, Mugetsu displays tremendous ...hysical abilities and superhuman strength. What has this crazed fanatic ...ndergone to gain such unique fighting abilities? Mugetsu attacks the ...ar FATE with his team and kidnaps Dominique.

UNLOCKING MUGETSU

...o unlock Mugetsu with Mask in Versus and Survival Modes, you must ...efeat him in Battle 10 of Story Mode in the Hanging Garden area. You ...an unlock Mugetsu without Mask by defeating him in Battle 24 on the ...ir-Carrier. His Rank improves each time you defeat him in Extra Games, ...epending on your overall Game Rank. Each of Mugetsu's two forms has ...ifferent moves and skill levels.

ALTERNATE COSTUMES

Mugetsu with Mask 1.
(R2 Button)

Mugetsu with Mask 2.
(L1 Button)

Mugetsu with Mask 3.
(L2 Button)

MUGETSU WITH MASK STATUS CHART

Status	Rank							
	G	F	E	D	C	B	A	S
Life	110	124	138	152	167	181	195	210
Power	90	105	121	137	152	168	184	200
Defense	70	84	98	112	127	141	155	170
BP	150	200	250	300	350	400	450	600

AVAILABLE EXTRA SKILLS

Skill Name	Rank							
	G	F	E	D	C	B	A	S
Ren-Getsu	-	-	*	*	*	*	*	*
Gen-Getsu (Hell)	*	*	*	*	*	*	*	*
Gen-Getsu (Heaven)	*	*	*	*	*	*	*	*
Hi-Getsu	-	-	-	*	*	*	*	*

MUGETSU WITH MASK MOVES LIST

Type	Name	Command	Base Damage
Jump	Forward Flip Kick	j	12
Jump	Assault Spin Kick	J	22
High	Jab	h	8
High	Straight Chop	h,h	10
High	Heel Drop	h,h,h	14
High	Final Stroke	h,h,H	21
High	Rising Back Kick	H	15
High	Side Kick	H,h	17
High	Flying Kick	Direction + h	35
Middle	Reverse Chop	m	8
Middle	Double Reverse Chop	m,m	13
Middle	Triple Reverse Chop	m,m,m	18
Middle	Heartstopper (Right)	m,m,M	20

Type	Name	Command	Base Damage
Middle	Tumble Kick	M	13
Middle	Corkscrew Kick	M,m	18
Middle	Heartstopper (Left)	m,M	24
Low	Low Kick	l	8
Low	Low Reverse Kick	l,l	9
Low	Low Reverse Chop	l,l,L	22
Low	Sweep	L	12
ES1	Ren-Getsu	ES + m	15
	2nd hit	ES + m (x2)	27
ES2	Gen-Getsu (Hell)	ES + l	25
ES3	Gen-Getsu (Heaven)	ES + h	25
ES4	Hi-Getsu*	ES + j	-
	(Hi-Getsu-Rush)	ES + j (x2)	22

*The first "hit" is a backflip that doesn't cause damage.

ALTERNATE COSTUMES

Mugetsu without Mask 1. (R2 Button)

Mugetsu without Mask 2. (L1 Button)

Mugetsu without Mask 3. (L2 Button)

MUGETSU WITHOUT MASK STATUS CHART

Status	Rank							
	G	F	E	D	C	B	A	S
Life	120	134	148	162	177	191	205	220
Power	100	115	131	147	162	178	194	210
Defense	65	79	93	107	122	136	150	165
BP	180	240	300	360	420	480	540	720

AVAILABLE EXTRA SKILLS

Skill Name	Rank							
	G	F	E	D	C	B	A	S
Shi-Getsu	-	*	*	*	*	*	*	*
Fuku-Getsu	-	-	-	-	*	*	*	*
Ka-Getsu	-	-	*	*	*	*	*	*
Ren-Getsu	*	*	*	*	*	*	*	*

MUGETSU WITHOUT MASK MOVES LIST

Type	Name	Command	Base Damage
Jump	Forward Flip Kick	j	13
Jump	Crazy Hammer	J	27
High	Crazy Jab	h	7
High	Crazy Hook	h,h	10
High	Crazy Back Kick	h,h,h	21
High	Crazy Elbow	h,h,H	16
High	Crazy High Kick	H	15
Middle	Crazy Chop	m	12
Middle	Crazy Uppercut	m,m	18
Middle	Crazy Knee	M	22
Middle	Crazy Straight Chop	m,M	21
Middle	Crazy Drill	Direction + m	22

Type	Name	Command	Base Damage
Low	Crazy Low Kick	l	12
Low	Crazy Sweep	l,L	20
ES1	Shi-Getsu	ES + m	20
	2nd hit	ES + m (x2)	32
ES2	Fuku-Getsu*	ES + l	-
	2nd hit	ES + l (x2)	29
ES3	Ka-Getsu**	ES + h	10
	2nd hit	ES + h (x2)	24
ES4	Ren-Getsu	ES + h + m	10

*The first "hit" is a feint.

**Throw move (first hit).

DOMINIQUE CROSS

Age: 15   Height: 4'10"   Fighting Style: Custom

[fri]ghtened, alone and abandoned, Dominique Cross was rescued by Sion, [wh]o found her in the middle of town. Dominique is a bright and friendly [yo]ung girl who has quickly become the mascot for FATE, the bar in which [the] bouncers work. Having endeared herself to them all, Sion and the [oth]er bouncers are willing to risk their lives for her.

UNLOCKING DOMINIQUE

[Yo]u can unlock Dominique after all the PD-4 units have been destroyed in [th]e Rocket Tower. Her Rank and available Extra Skills depend upon the [pla]yer's Game Rank at that time.

ALTERNATE COSTUMES

Dominique 2. (R2 Button)   Yellow Raincoat. (L1 Button)   Peach Raincoat. (L2 Button)

DOMINIQUE'S STATUS CHART

Status	Rank							
	G	F	E	D	C	B	A	S
Life	60	71	82	94	105	117	128	140
Power	120	139	158	177	197	216	235	255
Defense	50	68	87	105	124	142	161	180
BP	0	0	0	0	0	0	0	0

AVAILABLE EXTRA SKILLS

Skill Name	Rank							
	G	F	E	D	C	B	A	S
Spike Bomber	-	-	*	*	*	*	*	*
Linear Drive	-	-	-	*	*	*	*	*
Rolling Power Throw	-	-	-	-	*	*	*	*
Destruction Uppercut	-	-	-	-	-	-	*	*

DOMINIQUE'S MOVES LIST

Type	Name	Command	Base Damage
Jump	Dominique Spin Drop	j	21
Jump	Dominique Somersault Twist	J	25
High	Dominique Punch	h	8
High	Dominique Straight Punch	h,h	12
High	Side Kick	h,h,h	16
High	Rising Spin Kick	H	26
High	Power Spin Punch	h,H	22

Type	Name	Command	Base Damage
Middle	Body Punch	m	12
Middle	Scorpion Kick	M	12
Middle	Ground Spin Kick	M,m	15
Middle	Ground Spin Kick 2	M,m,m	15
Middle	Spinning Body Blow	m,M	24
Middle	Dominique Bounce	Direction + m	26
Low	Toe Kick	l	10
Low	Slide Kick	L	12
Low	Squat Kick	l,L	20
ES1	Spike Bomber	ES + j	29
ES2	Linear Drive*	ES + m	34
ES3	Rolling Power Throw*	ES + l	28
ES4	Destruction Uppercut	ES + h	31

*Throw moves.

PD-4

Age: ??   Height: 5'11"   Fighting Style: Muay Tai

[H]umanoid fighting weapons developed by Mikado, PD-4s are equipped [wi]th the mysterious bionoid technology. Because they are prototypes, [th]ere are very few operational units. They speak in a cold, mechanical, [and] male tone of voice.

UNLOCKING PD-4

[To] unlock PD-4, you must defeat the unit in Battle 21 in the Rocket Tower [B]asement. Its Rank and Extra Skills are dependent upon your overall [G]ame Rank and are improved each time you defeat it.

ALTERNATE COSTUMES

PD-4 1. (R2 Button)   PD-4 2. (L1 Button)   PD-4 3. (L2 Button)

PD-4'S STATUS CHART

Status	Rank							
	G	F	E	D	C	B	A	S
Life	120	134	148	162	177	191	205	220
Power	90	102	115	128	141	154	167	180
Defense	95	107	120	133	146	159	172	185
BP	170	226	283	340	396	453	510	680

AVAILABLE EXTRA SKILLS

Skill Name	Rank							
	G	F	E	D	C	B	A	S
Thunder Fall	-	-	*	*	*	*	*	*
Lightning Whip	*	*	*	*	*	*	*	*
Elbow Spin Break	*	*	*	*	*	*	*	*
Lightning Viper	-	-	-	*	*	*	*	*

PD-4'S MOVES LIST

Type	Name	Command	Base Damage
Jump	Feint	j	19
Jump	Swaying	j,j	20
Jump	Fading Knee	j,j,j	27
Jump	Spinning Fan	J	23
Jump	Combo Punch	Direction + j	22
High	Jab	h	6
High	Combo Punch	h,h	8
High	Elbow Punch	h,h,h	8
High	Cross Elbow	h,h,H	22
High	Roundhouse	h,h,h,h	8
High	Right Cross	h,h,h,H	20
High	Arm Whip	h,h,h,h,H	19
High	Roundhouse	H	15
High	Crescent Kick	H,h	17
High	Uppercut	h,H	25
Middle	Body Blow	m	8
Middle	Double Body Blow	m,m	10
Middle	Straight Punch (Right)	m,m,m	18
Middle	Forward Kick	M	12

Type	Name	Command	Base Damage
Middle	Shin Splint*	M,m	6
		M,m,m	6
		M,m,m,m	6
		M,m,m,m,m	6
		M,m,m,m,m,m	10
Middle	High Spin Kick	M,m,m,m,m,m,m	15
Middle	Knee Thrust	m,M	26
Low	Inside Toe Kick	l	12
Low	Trip Kick	L	18
Low	Double Trip Kick	l,L	15
ES1	Thunder Fall**	ES + h	25
ES2	Lightning Whip	ES + m	25
ES3	Elbow Spin Break	ES + l	20
	2nd hit	ES + l (x2)	36
ES4	Lightning Viper**	ES + h + m	32

*By repeatedly pressing the Middle attack button, the player can repeatedly kick to the mid-section of the opponent.
**Unblockable attacks.

KALDEA ORCHID

Age: Unknown   Height: 5'5"   Fighting Style: Transcendental

A beautiful but silent woman who is always by Dauragon's side, Kaldea's expression indicates a certain degree of sadness in her. Perhaps she feels sorry for Dauragon, since she seems to be the only one who truly understands him.

UNLOCKING KALDEA

You can unlock Kaldea in Versus and Survival Modes by defeating her in the Galeos Passageway in Battle 25. Her Rank and Extra Skills are improved each time you fight her, depending upon your overall Game Rank.

ALTERNATE COSTUMES

Lavender Costume. (R2 Button)

Sexy Black Outfit. (L1 Button)

Sexy White Outfit. (L2 Button)

KALDEA'S STATUS CHART

	Rank							
Status	G	F	E	D	C	B	A	S
Life	100	113	127	140	154	167	181	195
Power	70	84	98	112	127	141	155	170
Defense	90	105	121	137	152	168	184	200
BP	120	160	200	240	280	320	360	480

AVAILABLE EXTRA SKILLS

	Rank							
Skill Name	G	F	E	D	C	B	A	S
Griffin Talons	-	-	*	*	*	*	*	*
Meteor Storm	*	*	*	*	*	*	*	*
Griffin Tail	-	-	-	-	*	*	*	*
Spinning Rush	*	*	*	*	*	*	*	*
Wild Fang	-	-	-	*	*	*	*	*
Shape Shift	*	*	*	*	*	*	*	*

KALDEA'S MOVES LIST

Type	Name	Command	Base Damage
Jump	Spinning Fan	j	23
High	Jab	h	8
High	Reverse Chop	h,h	10
High	Back High Kick	h,h,h	15
High	Griffon Fang	H	22
High	Wing Punch	H,h	17
High	Roundhouse Kick	h,H	20
Middle	Middle Thrust	m	18
Middle	Short Uppercut	m,m	15
Middle	Straight Punch	M	25
Middle	Griffon Launcher	m,M	10

Type	Name	Command	Base Damage
Low	Inside Kick	l	8
Low	Reverse Spin Kick	l,l	9
Low	Low Reverse Chop	l,l,l	14
Low	Double Palm Thrust	L	24
ES1	Griffin Talons	ES + j	18
ES2	Meteor Storm*	ES + h	14
	2nd hit		9
	3rd hit		8
	4th hit		7
	5th hit		24
ES3	Griffin Tail	ES + m	20
	2nd hit	ES + m (x2)	35
ES4	Shape Shift	ES + l	-

*All 5 hits are executed when the move is successfully performed against an enemy.

KALDEA'S PANTHER FORM MOVES LIST

Type	Name	Command	Base Damage
Jump	Jump Scratch	j	17
Jump	Tail Drop	J	26
High	High Scratch	h	12
High	High Dash Attack	H	24
Middle	Panther Toss	m	13
Middle	Middle Dash Attack	M	21

Type	Name	Command	Base Damage
Low	Low Scratch	l	11
Low	Tail Attack	L	15
ES1	Spinning Rush	ES + h	15
ES2	Wild Fang*	ES + m	23
ES3	Shape Shift	ES + l	-

*Throw move.

HIDDEN CHARACTERS

DAURAGON C. MIKADO

Age: 26   Height: 6'2"   Fighting Style: Open-Hand Dragon Prayer

young leader of the massive multinational Mikado Group Corporation, ragon only recently ascended to his current position. He is the adopted son of previous leader. Dauragon has rigorously trained both mind and body, knowing he would one day lead the company.

pite of his good fortune, he reigns as a cold-hearted leader, calm and collect- regardless of the circumstances. The mastermind behind the kidnapping of ninique, his true motives for doing so are unveiled only as the story unfolds.

UNLOCKING DAURAGON

cause you fight the mind behind Mikado several times in the game, he has four ms that you can unlock for use in Versus and Survival Modes. One-armed ragon, who fights with only one hand, is unlocked after defeating him in Battle of Story Mode. Normal Dauragon is the first form of final Boss Dauragon; to ck him, you must defeat him in Battle 26. You can unlock Overalls Dauragon winning Battle 27. Lastly, to unlock Shirtless Dauragon, you must clear Story de three times.

ALTERNATE COSTUMES

One-Armed Dauragon in white. (R2 Button)

One-Armed Dauragon in gold. (L1 Button)

One-Armed Dauragon in yellow. (L2 Button)

ONE-ARMED DAURAGON'S STATUS CHART

	Rank							
Status	G	F	E	D	C	B	A	S
Life	120	134	148	162	177	191	205	220
Power	70	88	107	125	144	162	181	200
Defense	70	82	95	108	121	134	147	160
BP	110	146	183	220	256	293	330	440

AVAILABLE EXTRA SKILLS

	Rank							
Skill Name	G	F	E	D	C	B	A	S
Whirlwind Kick	*	*	*	*	*	*	*	*
Crescent Moon Slash	*	*	*	*	*	*	*	*
Triple Rave Kick	-	-	-	-	*	*	*	*
Elbow Spear	-	-	*	*	*	*	*	*

ONE-ARMED DAURAGON'S MOVES LIST

Type	Name	Command	Base Damage
Jump	Spinning Fan	j	20
Jump	Forward Jump Kick	J	15
Jump	Talon Kick	Direction + j	12
Jump	Double Talon Kick	Direction + j (x2)	15
High	Jab	h	11
High	Spin Kick	H	16
High	Striking Blow	h,H	25
Middle	Uppercut	m	12
Middle	Fading Elbow	M	21
Middle	Down Thrust	m,M	20

Type	Name	Command	Base Damage
Low	Sweep	l	9
Low	Reverse Sweep	L	14
Low	Double Sweep	l,L	21
ES1	Whirlwind Kick	ES + m	16
ES2	Crescent Moon Slash	ES + j	12-18
ES3	Triple Rave Kick	ES + h	13
		ES + h (x2)	16
		ES + h (x3)	20
ES4	Elbow Spear	ES + h + m	21

ALTERNATE COSTUMES

Normal Dauragon in gold.
(L1 Button)

Normal Dauragon in white.
(R2 Button)

Normal Dauragon in yellow.
(L2 Button)

NORMAL DAURAGON'S STATUS CHART

Status	Rank							
	G	F	E	D	C	B	A	S
Life	125	140	155	170	185	200	215	230
Power	80	97	114	131	148	165	182	200
Defense	80	94	108	122	137	151	165	180
BP	150	200	250	300	350	400	450	600

AVAILABLE EXTRA SKILLS

Skill Name	Rank							
	G	F	E	D	C	B	A	S
Whirlwind Kick	*	*	*	*	*	*	*	*
Crescent Moon Slash	*	*	*	*	*	*	*	*
Dragon Claw	-	*	*	*	*	*	*	*
Dragon Blitz	*	*	*	*	*	*	*	*
Wyvern's Sting	-	-	-	-	*	*	*	*

NORMAL DAURAGON'S MOVES LIST

Type	Name	Command	Base Damage
Jump	Spinning Fan	j	20
Jump	Forward Jump Kick	J	11
Jump	Double Forward Kick	J,j	19
Jump	Talon Kick	Direction + j	12
Jump	Double Talon Kick	Direction + j(x2)	17
High	Palm Strike	h	12
High	Dragon Fang	h,h	10
High	Dragon Frenzy	h,h,h	21
High	Spin Kick	H	16
High	Striking Palm	h,H	20

*Throw move (first hit).

Type	Name	Command	Base Damage
Middle	Double Palm Blow	m	16
Middle	Double Palm Strike	M	15
Middle	Dragon Wing	m,M	22
Low	Sweep	l	8
Low	Reverse Sweep	L	12
Low	Double Sweep	l,L	26
ES1	Whirlwind Kick	ES + m	16
ES2	Crescent Moon Slash	ES + j	12-18
ES3	Dragon Claw	ES + h	25
ES4	Dragon Blitz	ES + h + m	36
ES5	Wyvern's Sting*	ES + h + j	10
	2nd hit		20

ALTERNATE COSTUMES

Overalls Dauragon 1.
(R2 Button)

Overalls Dauragon 2.
(L1 Button)

Overalls Dauragon 3.
(L2 Button)

OVERALLS DAURAGON'S STATUS CHART

Status	Rank							
	G	F	E	D	C	B	A	S
Life	130	145	160	175	190	205	220	235
Power	100	114	128	142	157	171	185	200
Defense	100	112	125	138	151	164	177	190
BP	220	293	366	440	513	586	660	880

AVAILABLE EXTRA SKILLS

Skill Name	Rank							
	G	F	E	D	C	B	A	S
Sonic Elbow	*	*	*	*	*	*	*	*
Dragon Spiral	*	*	*	*	*	*	*	*
Launcher	-	-	*	*	*	*	*	*
Jet Uppercut	-	-	-	-	*	*	*	*

OVERALLS DAURAGON'S MOVES LIST

Type	Name	Command	Base Damage
Jump	Spinning Fan	j	20
Jump	Forward Jump Kick	J	11
Jump	Double Forward Kick	J,j	19
Jump	Talon Kick	Direction + j	12
Jump	Double Talon Kick	Direction + j(x2)	17
High	Palm Strike	h	12
High	Dragon Fang	h,h	10
High	Dragon Frenzy	h,h,h	21
High	Spin Kick	H	16
High	Striking Palm	h,H	20

Type	Name	Command	Base Damage
Middle	Double Palm Blow	m	16
Middle	Double Palm Strike	M	15
Middle	Dragon Wing	m,M	22
Middle	Lunging Strike	Direction + m	21
Low	Sweep	l	8
Low	Reverse Sweep	L	12
Low	Double Sweep	l,L	26
ES1	Sonic Elbow	ES + m	18
ES2	Dragon Elbow	ES + l	20
ES3	Launcher	ES + j	15-25
ES4	Jet Uppercut*	ES + m + l	38

*Unblockable attack.

ALTERNATE COSTUMES

Shirtless Dauragon 1.
(L1 Button)

Shirtless Dauragon 2.
(R2 Button)

Shirtless Dauragon 3.
(L2 Button)

SHIRTLESS DAURAGON'S STATUS CHART

	Rank							
Status	G	F	E	D	C	B	A	S
Life	150	165	180	195	210	225	240	255
Power	100	115	131	147	162	178	194	210
Defense	85	97	109	121	133	145	157	170
BP	350	466	583	700	816	933	1050	1400

AVAILABLE EXTRA SKILLS

	Rank							
Skill Name	G	F	E	D	C	B	A	S
Sonic Elbow	*	*	*	*	*	*	*	*
Dragon Spiral	*	*	*	*	*	*	*	*
Flying Dragon Kick	-	-	*	*	*	*	*	*
Rushing Beat	-	-	-	-	*	*	*	*

SHIRTLESS DAURAGON'S MOVES LIST

Type	Name	Command	Base Damage
Jump	Spinning Fan	j	20
Jump	Forward Jump Kick	J	11
Jump	Double Forward Kick	J,j	19
High	Palm Strike	h	12
High	Dragon Fang	h,h	10
High	Dragon Frenzy	h,h,h	21
High	Spin Kick	H	16
High	Striking Palm	h,H	20
Middle	Double Palm Blow	m	16
Middle	Double Palm Strike	M	15
Middle	Dragon Wing	m,M	22
Middle	Lunging Strike	Direction + m	21

Type	Name	Command	Base Damage
Low	Sweep	l	8
Low	Reverse Sweep	L	12
Low	Double Sweep	l,L	26
ES1	Sonic Elbow	ES + m	18
ES2	Dragon Spiral	ES + l	20
ES3	Flying Dragon Kick	ES + j	12-18
ES4	Rushing Beat*	ES + m + l	6
	2nd hit		7
	3rd hit		8
	4th hit		8
	5th hit		9
	6th hit		12
	7th hit		6
	8th hit		8
	9th hit		7
	10th hit		18

*All 10 hits are executed when the move is performed.

WONG LEUNG

Age: Unknown Height: Unknown Fighting Style: Open-Palm Dragon-Pray

Master Wong is a loyal member of the Mikado family, having served under the previous CEO. Prior to his engagement at the Mikado Group, he tutored both Dauragon and Sion, training them both in the martial arts. He may look stern and uptight, but he is a man of character. He is quite troubled by whatever it is that Dauragon is planning…

ALTERNATE COSTUMES

Wong 1. (R2 Button) Wong 2. (L2 Button) Wong 3. (L1 Button)

UNLOCKING MASTER WONG

You must use either Volt or Kou to infiltrate the Mikado Building and to defeat the Black Panther onboard the Galeos. Then use Sion to defeat Dauragon. During the Epilogue, Sion will flash back to his training with Wong. After defeating Wong, he will appear in Versus and Survival Modes. His Rank and Extra Skills are dependent upon the overall Game Rank of your saved game.

WONG'S STATUS CHART

Status	Rank							
	G	F	E	D	C	B	A	S
Life	100	111	122	134	145	157	168	180
Power	110	126	142	159	175	192	208	225
Defense	100	111	122	134	145	157	168	180
BP	120	160	200	240	280	320	360	480

AVAILABLE EXTRA SKILLS

Skill Name	Rank							
	G	F	E	D	C	B	A	S
Step-In Elbow	-	-	-	*	*	*	*	*
Vertical Smasher	*	*	*	*	*	*	*	*
Launcher	*	*	*	*	*	*	*	*
Cross Break	-	*	*	*	*	*	*	*
Silent Exploder	-	-	-	-	*	*	*	*
Wyvern's Charge	-	-	-	-	*	*	*	*

WONG'S MOVES LIST

Type	Name	Command	Base Damage
Jump	Spinning Fan	j	22
Jump	Forward Jump Kick	J	12
High	Palm Strike	h	10
High	Dragon Claw	h,h	11
High	Dragon Rage	h,h,h	15
High	Dragon Blitz	H	22
High	Striking Palm	h,H	20
Middle	Double Palm Blow	m	11
Middle	Elbow Strike	M	18
Middle	Dragon Wing	m,M	20

Type	Name	Command	Base Damage
Low	Sweep	l	10
Low	Reverse Sweep	L	14
Low	Double Sweep	l,L	18
ES1	Step-In Elbow	ES + h	32
ES2	Vertical Smasher	ES + m	25
ES3	Launcher	ES + l	26
ES4	Cross Break	ES + m + l	20
	2nd hit		36
ES5	Silent Exploder	ES + h + m	70
ES6	Wyvern's Charge*	ES + h + j	10
	2nd hit		20

*Throw move (first hit).

LEANN CALDWELL

Age: Classified! Height: 5'6" Fighting Style: Cutting Fist

A mysterious agent with some interest in Dominique and Mikado, Leann's actions and motivations are secretive. Duty-bound and strong willed, Leann carries out her missions with the utmost precaution and planning.

ALTERNATE COSTUMES

Leann alternate color. (R2 Button) Leann in white bathrobe. (L2 Button) Leann in blue bath... (L1 Button)

UNLOCKING LEANN

You must use Kou to infiltrate the Mikado building and defeat Dauragon, after which Kou will encounter Leann during his Epilogue and be forced to fight her. (See Ending Event Sequence in the "Secrets" section of the **Story Mode** chapter.)

After defeating her in battle, Leann will be unlocked for use in Versus and Survival Modes. Her Rank and available Extra Skills are dependent upon the player's overall Game Rank, as recorded in the saved game.

LEANN'S STATUS CHART

Status	Rank							
	G	F	E	D	C	B	A	S
Life	105	118	132	145	159	172	186	200
Power	95	107	120	133	146	159	172	185
Defense	110	123	137	150	164	177	191	205
BP	120	160	200	240	280	320	360	480

AVAILABLE EXTRA SKILLS

Skill Name	Rank							
	G	F	E	D	C	B	A	S
Shuriken Kick	*	*	*	*	*	*	*	*
Rising Spinner	-	-	*	*	*	*	*	*
Shoulder Slam	-	*	*	*	*	*	*	*
Somersault Edge	-	-	-	-	*	*	*	*

LEANN'S MOVES LIST

Type	Name	Command	Base Damage
Jump	Twin Blade	j	13
Jump	Assault Kick*	J	12-18
High	Lead Jab	h	8
High	Double Jab	h,h	9
High	Triple Jab	h,h,h	13
High	High Kick	H	12
High	Middle Back Kick	H,h	12
High	Combo High Kick	H,h,h	15
High	Back Knuckle	h,H	24
High	Side Spin Kick	run + h	15
Middle	Tower Kick	m	8
Middle	Side Step Kick	M	27

Type	Name	Command	Base Damage
Middle	Somersault Combo	m,M	18
Middle	Jumping Side Kick	Direction + m	19
Low	Low Step	l	10
Low	Backside Low Kick	L	16
Low	Waterline Spin Kick	l,L	18
Low	Short Slide Kick	Direction + l	14
ES1	Shuriken Kick	ES + h	16-23
ES2	Rising Spinner	ES + j	11-17
ES3	Shoulder Slam**	ES + m	24
ES4	Somersault Edge	ES + j + h	23

*The second hit will graze the enemy.
**Throw move.

REGULAR ENEMIES

The following are status charts and moves lists for the regular enemies that you fight throughout the game. It should be noted that you cannot unlock these enemies in Versus or Survival Modes. Also, regular enemies do not learn Extra Skills. The amount of BP earned by defeating them is based upon the player's overall Game Rank. Moves lists have been included to warn you of the damage an enemy is capable of inflicting.

MSF (MIKADO SPECIAL FORCES)

MSF STATUS CHART

Status	Rank							
	G	F	E	D	C	B	A	S
Life	60	71	83	95	106	118	130	200
Power	55	74	93	112	131	150	170	210
Defense	40	56	73	90	106	123	140	170
BP	25	33	41	50	58	66	75	0

MSF ELITE

MSF ELITE STATUS CHART

Status	Rank							
	G	F	E	D	C	B	A	S
Life	75	87	100	112	125	137	150	230
Power	65	85	106	127	148	169	190	240
Defense	45	62	80	97	115	132	150	180
BP	40	53	66	80	93	106	120	0

CARRIER SOLDIER

CARRIER SOLDIER STATUS CHART

Status	Rank							
	G	F	E	D	C	B	A	S
Life	50	60	70	80	90	100	110	160
Power	50	68	86	105	123	141	160	200
Defense	50	68	86	105	123	141	160	200
BP	35	46	58	70	81	93	105	0

SECURITY GUARD

SECURITY GUARD STATUS CHART

Status	Rank							
	G	F	E	D	C	B	A	S
Life	50	60	70	80	90	100	110	160
Power	45	62	80	97	115	132	150	200
Defense	45	62	80	97	115	132	150	200
BP	20	26	33	40	46	53	60	0

SECURITY CHIEF

SECURITY CHIEF STATUS CHART

Status	Rank							
	G	F	E	D	C	B	A	S
Life	60	71	83	95	106	118	130	170
Power	50	68	86	105	123	141	160	200
Defense	50	68	86	105	123	141	160	200
BP	30	40	50	60	70	80	90	0

COMMANDER

COMMANDER STATUS CHART

Status	Rank							
	G	F	E	D	C	B	A	S
Life	80	93	106	120	133	146	160	200
Power	55	74	93	112	131	150	170	210
Defense	60	80	100	120	140	160	180	220
BP	50	66	83	100	116	133	150	0

WATCHDOG (BAKILLA)

WATCHDOG STATUS CHART

Status	Rank							
	G	F	E	D	C	B	A	S
Life	35	45	56	67	78	89	100	150
Power	75	97	120	142	165	187	210	255
Defense	45	62	80	97	115	132	150	180
BP	30	40	50	60	70	80	90	0

P-101

P-101 STATUS CHART

Status	Rank							
	G	F	E	D	C	B	A	S
Life	80	94	108	122	137	151	165	180
Power	40	54	68	82	97	111	125	140
Defense	40	58	76	94	112	130	160	190
BP	35	52	70	87	105	122	140	0

MC-07

MC-07 STATUS CHART

Status	Rank							
	G	F	E	D	C	B	A	S
Life	120	135	151	167	182	198	214	230
Power	80	97	114	131	148	165	182	200
Defense	36	52	69	86	103	120	150	180
BP	45	60	75	90	105	120	135	0

LD-15

LD-15 STATUS CHART

Status	Rank							
	G	F	E	D	C	B	A	S
Life	140	156	172	189	205	222	238	255
Power	100	120	140	160	180	200	220	240
Defense	44	65	86	107	128	150	190	230
BP	60	80	100	120	140	160	180	0

LD-X1

LD-X1 STATUS CHART

Status	Rank							
	G	F	E	D	C	B	A	S
Life	150	165	180	195	210	225	240	255
Power	110	130	151	172	192	213	234	255
Defense	48	69	90	112	133	155	205	255
BP	100	133	166	200	233	266	300	0

THE BOUNCER INTERVIEW

INTERVIEW BY IGNPS2 • DOUGLASS C. PERRY • DAVID ZDYRKO • DAVID SMITH

Thanks to the folks at **IGNPS2**, we were lucky enough to include this interview they conducted with the Director of The Bouncer, **Takashi Tokita**.

Q: What was the original idea behind The Bouncer?

A: The game is a synthesis of ideas from the development staff, but as a concept, it is a "playable action movie." Having three main characters lets you see the story from the perspective of your favorite one.

Q: Do you feel that you achieved what you set out to do with The Bouncer? Why?

A: I tend to focus on concept, so in that sense, I was able to achieve what I had originally set out to do. I believe I was able to achieve my goal by continually maintaining the concept without being affected by new hardware research/development, detailed animation sequences, and the creation of other detailed scenes.

Q: What do you think of the American voice acting compared to the Japanese voice acting?

A: Since we were considering a U.S. release from the beginning of the project, we started out with English voiceovers only. Japanese voiceovers were added later to provide more of a DVD quality to the game. Due to my acting experience and my 2-year stay in LA for the Parasite Eve production, the English voice recording seemed to flow smoothly without too many problems. The fact that the recording director was also an actor proved to be a helpful asset as well.

In Japan, the method of recording voices to fit the picture is considered mainstream, but for The Bouncer, we recorded the voices first and then created the (facial) animation to fit the voices. This method seemed to improve the quality of the voice acting.

Q: The graphic special effects in The Bouncer are quite amazing. How did you create the glossy filter and what did you try to achieve with it?

A: No matter how many polygons you use or how realistic the textures are, without filters and lighting, CG pictures will be of a quality lower than that of a figurine.

In order to create atmosphere, we spent much time on filters and lighting. We adjusted each scene in detail with an editor that conducts parameter adjustments on the actual hardware.

Q: What kinds of influences did you draw upon when you created the unusual and beautiful characters?

A: I've been inspired by the images that character designer Tetsuya Nomura has drawn. His ideas have influenced me a lot, but I believe that the time I spent acting before I joined Square has provided great inspiration as well.

In game production, you have to be an actor, a choreographer, a scenario writer, and more in order to create deep characters.

Q: Which is your favorite character to play and why?

A: I personally prefer Kou Leifoh. Sion is the standard main character type while Volt is a cool, silent, mature man. Kou is the comic relief, but he also has the most difficult mission to live up to. I believe that video games benefit greatly by having both serious and comical elements.

Q: There appear to be more than three endings in The Bouncer. How many are there, and what kinds of things will gamers discover by finishing the game many times?

A: In a broad sense, yes, there are three endings from the standpoint of seeing the perspectives of the three characters, but there are also minor branches within each ending.

In addition to the three endings, there are also about 9 variations in the epilogue sequence. Branching can occur after playing several times, or may occur with the timing of selecting characters, so I hope players enjoy the variations by playing the game more than three times.

Q: Do you have a favorite special move in the game? Which is it and why?

A: I especially like Volt's throwing technique called "Power Bridge." Depending on the grasping angle, you can watch a suplex that is different when seen from the front, side, and back. I am personally a big WWF fan (my favorite wrestler is "THE GAME." HHH!).

Q: Ehrgeiz was a very different direction for Dreamfactory. Do you feel that The Bouncer is more of a direct descendant of the Tobal series or Ehrgeiz?

A: Direction-wise, I believe it developed from Ehrgeiz. The basic control for follows the Tobal series.

Q: How often did you go to bars and research this game. Is there any kind of moral tale you're trying to tell about bouncers?

A: I enjoy going to bars during my free time, so I've never actually gone for the sake of research (laughs). During my stay in LA, I often visited bars with bouncers.

In the game, the three bouncers are not just throwing their weight around because it's their job; they've all had different pasts and circumstances that led them to become bouncers. Selecting the character and following the main story reveals the course of their life. I wanted to express the true strength and sincerity that lies beneath a strong exterior.

Q: How did you decide to choose the camera angles in The Bouncer? Do you feel that they work well? Why?

A: I first determine general camera angles with storyboards. Next, adjustments are made when the animations are created. After the animations are complete and displayed on the machine, then there are scenes that require further adjustment. Lastly, like editing a movie, adjustments are made after looking at the overall tempo.

The camera angles owe their success to the tools used in creating the animation and the system that allows interactive fine-tuning on the actual machine.

Q: What do you think of the PS2's 5.1 Dolby Digital sound? Was it a useful experiment and how do you feel it enhanced the game?

A: The effects of the 5.1 Dolby Digital Sound are used for the large scale FMVs. I believe this feature allows you to experience the atmosphere and intensity similar to that of a movie theater.

Q: Will there be a sequel to the Bouncer?

A: There are no plans at this time, but if it proves to be a big hit, we just might have to create a sequel, no matter what we say.

Q: The love story between Sion and Dominique is very unusual. Can you go into some detail as to how you thought up the story?

A: Yes, it is not a simple love story. With Sion, who has lost faith in human relationships, and with Dominique, who yearns for human relationships, their relationship is more of a family type of love rather than the traditional love between a man and a woman. The love between a man and a woman is something that ultimately forms a family.

The theme I concentrated on most was what Sion would do after learning Dominique's secret. This should become clear after viewing more than one ending. The song that is played during the ending credits is Dominique's answer to Sion.

BRAKES ARE FOR SISSIES.

DRIVING EMOTION TYPE-S™

Simulate the sensation of driving as closely as possible.

That was our goal. Technology has finally caught up with our ambition and racing will never be the same.
Everything, from the exterior and interior form and distinct behavior of the cars to the racing circuits,
has been painstakingly recreated using data provided by manufacturers and drivers.

DRIVING EMOTION TYPE-S
Setting the new standard for racing games.

Visit www.esrb.org or
call 1-800-771-3772
for Rating information.

PlayStation®2

PICK A WORLD
WE'LL TAKE YOU THERE

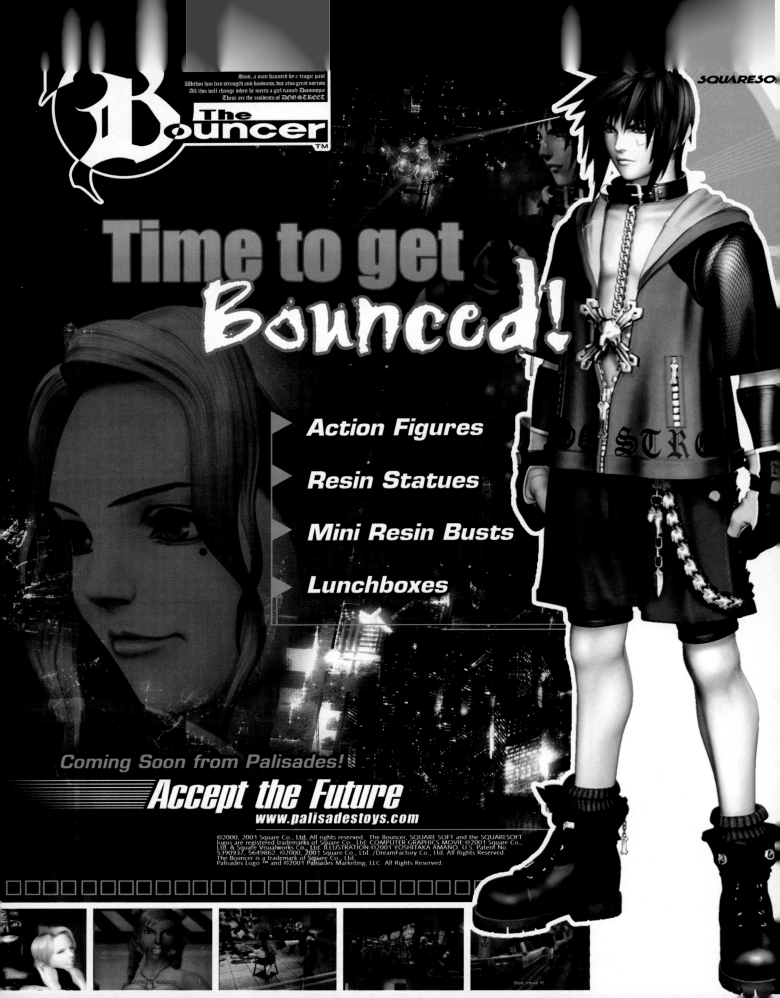